beaded weddings

beaded weddings

75+
Fabulous
Ideas

for Jewelry,
Invitations,
Reception Décor,
Gifts, and More

Jean Campbell

INTERWEAVE PRESS.

EDITOR: Rebecca Campbell
TECHNICAL EDITOR: Bonnie Brooks
PHOTOGRAPHY: Joe Coca
PHOTO STYLING: Ann Swanson and Paulette Livers
COVER AND INTERIOR DESIGN: Paulette Livers
ILLUSTRATIONS: Jason Reid
PRODUCTION: Pauline Brown
PROOFREADER AND INDEXER: Nancy Arndt

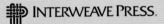 INTERWEAVE PRESS.

Interweave Press LLC
201 East Fourth Street
Loveland, CO 80537-5655 USA
www.interweave.com

Printed and bound in China by Asia Pacific.

Library of Congress Cataloging-in-Publication Data

Campbell, Jean, 1964-
  Beaded weddings : 75+ fabulous ideas for jewelry, invita-
tions, reception decor, gifts, and more / Jean Campbell, author.
    p. cm.
  Includes bibliographical references and index.
  ISBN-13: 978-1-931499-62-0
  ISBN-10: 931499-62-4
  1. Beadwork. 2. Wedding costume. 3. Dress accessories.
  4. Handicraft. I. Title.
  TT860 .C356
  745.58'2--dc22

                                    2006000745

10 9 8 7 6 5 4 3 2 1

acknowledgments

Thanks to the talented designers who contributed to *Beaded Weddings*: Arlene Baker, Nancy Dale, Jamie Hogsett, Jodi Reeb-Myers, and Dustin Wedekind. They each brought a creative voice to these pages, added spice and flavor to the book's concept, and provided much support for this old bead hand.

Thanks to the staff at Interweave Press. To Betsy Armstrong for our years-long brainstorming sessions that included the hatching of *Beaded Weddings*. To Rebecca Campbell, for her eagle eye, cracking whip, and witty ways. To Nancy Arndt for pouring over the words again and again and still smiling about it. To Jason Reid for his expert and beautiful illustrations, created in a lightning round. To Linda Stark and the Interweave Press marketing staff for bringing this book to you. To Paulette Livers for her impeccable graphic design and general stylistic flair. To Pauline Brown for putting this book together like a pro. And to Linda Ligon for creating a crafts book publishing monster.

Thanks to my family for putting up with my frenetic buzzing around the house while wearing red Converse All-Stars, sweats, and a beautiful tiara.

And finally, thanks to my dad, J. L. Cox, the king of all parties, who threw a fantastic celebration for us in 1989.

contents

introduction

Congratulations—you're getting married! There are stars in your eyes, the air is filled with love, and you have countless ideas for a picture-perfect wedding day. You envision sparkle, polish, glints of elegance, and beauty. But where to begin? Well, a little bead shopping isn't a bad place to start!

Bead shopping? At a time like this? Well, yes! Beads can make a gorgeous contribution to wedding-day pieces from your invitations to your gown. Beads can add drama and excitement on the big day—glistening bracelets and necklaces, bold centerpieces and cake toppers, and pretty invitations and thank-you notes are just some of the projects you can make with beads. Most bead projects work up amazingly quickly. The results are stunning, and you can usually save money by making your own pieces rather than buying them from commercial vendors.

Beaded Weddings is intended as both a how-to manual and an inspirational guide for brides who are looking for ways to make their wedding more personal, creative, and heartfelt. Each project includes step-by-step instructions, but you can easily add your own flavor to the mix. Beads are so versatile and varied that by simply changing shapes, types, and colors, you can adapt any project to suit your own wedding palette and style.

Just page through this book for inspiration! Before you know it, you'll be making wedding items that give your special day a unique, unforgettable style of its own.

Scheduling

Once you've decided that some beaded projects should be included in your wedding plans, the next thing you need to think about is scheduling. Most of the projects in this book can be made fairly quickly, but there are others you'll need to spend more time on, like a bag or woven bracelet. There are also projects you'll need to make multiples of (like invitations and table favors), which can eat up your time. And, although the air might be filled with cupid's arrows, it probably isn't filled with endless time or resources. Here are some ideas on getting those projects done.

💍 Fill a tray with enough beads and supplies for one project. Put the tray by the couch, so when you have some downtime you can begin beading where you left off. To avoid feeling overwhelmed, never put more than one project in the tray.

💍 Recruit moms, aunts, grandmas, sisters, friends, workmates, or anyone you know to assist you. You can even turn it into a fun event. Buy all the supplies for projects you'd like to make and throw a bead party. If your bridesmaids come, they can make their own wedding jewelry. Mom and grandma can make theirs, too. And your fiancé can help put together invitations and table favors.

☙ Count on help from your wedding planner, dressmaker, hairstylist, and florist for putting the finishing touches on your projects. You can get the ball rolling, and they can finish it up for you.

☙ Realize that you can't get it all done and ask for help! Prioritize your list of beaded wedding projects and work on them from the top down. What follows is a possible priority list, with an estimate of how long each project takes to make.

1. Embellish dress with beads (1 to 30 hours)
2. Make a headpiece (½ to 3 hours)
3. Create personal accessories (15 minutes for earrings to 30 hours for a purse)
4. Assemble invitations (½ hour to several hours)
5. Design bridesmaids' accessories (15 minutes to 2 hours)
6. Put together flower girl's accessories (1 to 4 hours)
7. Make beaded bouquet additions (½ hour to 6 hours)
8. Create cake topper and servers (1 to 6 hours)
9. Make a centerpiece (15 minutes to 5 hours)
10. Assemble table favors (2 minutes each)
11. Design thank-you notes (½ hour to several hours)
12. Create gifts for wedding party (½ hour to 5 hours)

O nce you leaf through the pages of this book and find a design you'd like to make, it's time to get down to business. Chances are you need a lesson or two to get started, so here's your Beading 101 class to set you on your way. Each project includes a materials and tools list. The techniques used are called out so you can come back to this section of the book to learn how to do it or to get a refresher if you've been beading for years.

Materials

Most of the materials used to make beaded wedding projects can be found at a bead or craft store. If not, I've given suggestions within the materials list for where to find them. You can also look on page 134 for a resource listing of specialty or hard-to-find products.

Beads

A nonbeader recently asked me how many kinds of beads there are in the world and if I had all of the different types. To put it plainly, the variety of beads is as vast as the makers, the countries they are made in, and the materials from which they are made. Plus, any one of those types of beads can come in different styles, colors, and patterns! These are all the reasons people get hooked on beading—there is always variety and excitement.

Since I don't have the luxury of giving you an overview of all the beads I can think of, here are some that you'll find in the project instructions. When you make your own projects, feel free to substitute other beads to fit your own style or to create personal meaning.

Bone beads. These inexpensive handmade beads are naturally white in color but can be easily dyed.

Bone beads

Charms. Charms come in a variety of shapes. Many depict favorite symbols or words. They are usually made of base or semiprecious metal and have a loop or hole on one side, so you can hang it from another finding. Charms are most often smaller than 1" or so. When they are larger than 1", they are called pendants.

Charms

Crystal beads. These leaded glass beads have crisp facets and a clean finish. The Austrian company, Swarovski, is the most recognizable brand of this type of bead.

Crystal beads

Fire-polished beads. This type of glass bead is made in the Czech Republic. They start as glass rounds and are then hand- or machine-faceted. A surface finish is often added to create extra sparkle. These work well as a less-expensive stand-in for crystals.

Fire-polished beads

India glass beads

Lampworked beads

Base metal beads

Silver- and gold-plated beads

Sterling silver beads

Gold-filled beads

Vermeil beads

India glass beads. These wound glass beads are a little rough around the edges but charming nonetheless. Because they are somewhat inexpensive, they work well for decorating projects.

Lampworked beads. Lampworked beads are created by an artist who hand-spins hot glass over a flame onto a mandrel. Because they are one-of-a-kind and can be rather expensive, you'll probably want to use them only in your wedding jewelry or as special gifts.

Metal beads. There are a variety of choices when you're buying metal beads. The least expensive, base metal beads, are comprised of nonprecious metals such as aluminum, brass, bronze, copper, and nickel. Silver- and 18k gold-plated beads, your next least-expensive option, are created by an electroplating process where a very thin layer of silver or gold is applied to another type of metal, like brass or copper. Sterling silver beads, the type suggested for use when you are making silver-based wedding jewelry, are a mix of silver and copper. For such silver to be sold legally as sterling, the percentages must be 92.5 percent pure silver and 7.5 percent copper. For those who would rather wear gold, choose gold-filled beads. They have $\frac{1}{10}$ of 12k gold applied to the surface of brass or another base metal. Another good option for those who like to wear gold is vermeil (pronounced vehr-MAY) beads. They are made of sterling silver electroplated with gold.

Pearls (freshwater). These beads are created by freshwater clams or mussels. Freshwater pearls have many surface irregularities, but that's part of their charm. When you're buying freshwater pearls, be careful to note where the drill holes are because many holes are off-center. Also test to see if your wire or other beading material passes through the holes of the pearls you buy because these beads have very small holes. It's possible to use a pearl reamer to make the holes larger, but it's much simpler to test the stringing material instead.

Freshwater pearls

Plastic beads. Plastic beads are lightweight and inexpensive. They come in a wide assortment of shapes, colors, and styles, as well as varying degrees of quality. Choose plastic beads that have little or no seam showing.

Plastic beads

Czech pressed-glass beads. These colorful and variously shaped molded glass beads are most often made in the Czech Republic, thus their nickname, "Czech glass."

Czech pressed-glass beads

Seed beads. These tiny beads are made by cutting long, thin canes of glass into little pieces. They are sized by number; the larger the number, the smaller the bead. For this book, you'll just need to use size 11° and size 14° seed beads. (That degree mark next to the size stands for "aught," a traditional beading term.) Bugle beads are long seed beads.

Semiprecious stone beads. Because there is a myriad of semiprecious stones, there is a myriad of semiprecious stone beads. They come in all sizes and shapes, but generally they are polished and faceted, donut-shaped, rough-cut, or chips. The holes in these beads are usually small, so test your stringing material to make sure the bead passes through.

Sequins. Sequins are flat pieces of pressed metal or plastic with a hole in the center or to one side. They're most commonly round and flat, but others are cut into shapes. Some are domed while others have patterns pressed into them. They are usually used to decorate fabric but make a fun addition to your beading stash.

Sequins

Findings

Findings are the commercially made metal pieces in your projects that help hook, connect, and secure your beads. There are just a few different types you'll need to use for the projects that follow.

Cell phone finding. This relatively newcomer to the family of findings is made up of a string attached to a tube attached to a heavy jump ring. You attach beaded dangles to the jump ring and thread the string through the hole on your cell phone, securing it with a lark's head knot. These findings can also be used to decorate other items such as zippers and purses.

Clasps. Clasps connect the ends of a necklace or bracelet. Some have one loop for single-strand pieces; others have two or more loops for multistranded pieces. You may be overwhelmed at the choices you have in clasps. If so, just go with the most simple-looking clasp.

Fishhook clasps are most commonly used with the classic pearl necklace. They have a hook on one end that catches into a marquise-shaped box.

Lobster and spring ring clasps have levers that open an internal spring after which they snap back shut. Attach this kind of clasp to a jump ring at the other end of the piece of jewelry.

Toggle clasps require tension from the weight of a necklace or the tightness of a bracelet to keep them shut. These clasps employ a ring and a bar; the bar passes through the ring on the perpendicular and closes when it's moved parallel.

Seed beads   Bugle beads

Semiprecious stone beads

Cell phone finding

Fishhook clasp

Lobster and spring ring clasp

Toggle clasp

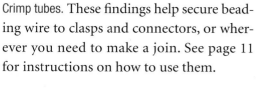

Crimp tubes. These findings help secure beading wire to clasps and connectors, or wherever you need to make a join. See page 11 for instructions on how to use them.

Earring findings. These are the pieces of metal that make the connection between your beadwork and your ear. There are several different styles, including clip-ons (for non-pierced ears); French ear wires (J-shaped); and posts (made up of a straight piece of wire with a stopper on one end and an ear nut on the other). All of these styles have loops that you can open like a jump ring. Open the ring, add the beaded dangle, and close the ring.

French wire (or gimp). This type of tiny coiled strand of wire is used to cover wires or thread.

Head pins. Head pins are straight pieces of wire with a small stopper at one end. They are often used for making earrings or other dangles.

Crimp tubes

Earring findings

French ear wires

Knot cups. These findings are meant for transitioning a soft fiber, like silk cord, to another metal finding like a clasp. To use, make a strong, thick knot in the fiber and string it through the knot cup from the inside out. Use pliers to close the cup. String your beads, and when you reach the end, pass the fiber through a second knot cup from the outside in. Make a strong, thick knot, and close the cup.

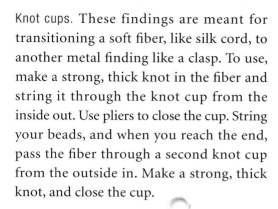

Knot cups

Rings. These are small circles of wire that connect pieces of beadwork. Jump rings open so you can add another finding or wire. To open, don't bend the ends away from each other but bend laterally. Soldered rings look like jump rings but have no opening. Split rings are shaped like tiny key rings.

Rings

Spacer bars. These findings keep multiple strands of jewelry separate and tidy.

Head pins

Spacer bars

Wire

Wire can seem like a lowly cousin when you go to the store to pick up your supplies. But it isn't! Wire is an all-important member of the family because it often serves as the backbone of your project. And in *Beaded Weddings* it's even more so because the majority of projects require wire. When working with wire, don't skimp—there's nothing more frustrating than running out of wire mid-project, especially if the big day is right around the corner.

Beading wire (brand names Accuflex, Acculon, Beadalon, Soft Flex). This is a very flexible nylon-coated multistrand steel wire available at virtually every bead shop. It comes in a variety of diameters—you're usually safe to buy the medium-width wire, but you'll want to be sure it will fit through your beads.

Craft wire. Craft wire is usually made out of a copper or brass alloy and has a plastic-coated surface. These wires come in a variety of colors, as well as a silver-plated version that resembles sterling silver wire.

Memory wire. Memory wire is made of tough, permanently coiled steel. It is so strong that you have to use heavy-duty cutters to cut it (it will mar the blade of small wire cutters). You can also break memory wire by bending it back and forth many times with pliers. Memory wire comes in necklace, bracelet, and ring widths.

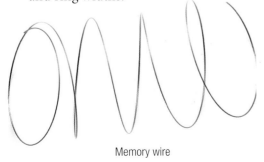

Memory wire

Thread

There is only a smattering of projects in this book that require thread. For those that do, make sure you secure your threads with strong knots, and if possible, weave through the beads as many times as possible. You'd hate for one of your special handmade projects to come undone mid-ceremony!

Braided thread or line. Braided thread (brand names Dandy Line and PowerPro) is an extremely strong synthetic thread that's also used for fishing. It has great strength (10–20 pound test), is very thin (.006 mm diameter), can be knotted, and comes in two colors: moss green and white. The angle of the blades on children's Fiskars scissors makes them most appropriate for cutting braided thread.

Nylon beading thread. Nylon beading thread (brand names C-Lon and Nymo) is thin synthetic thread that you purchase by the spool like regular sewing thread. Nylon is best used for lightweight stringing projects that require a needle and thread. Pre-stretch this material (pull the ends apart several times) before you use it.

Silk cord. This stringing material comes in almost every imaginable color. Sold on a spool or a card, it is sized by thickness: 00, 0, A, B, C, D, E, F, FF, and FFF, with 00 being the thinnest. Silk cord is often used for knotting pearl beads. It will stretch, so pre-stretching is advised.

Beading wire

Craft wire

Braided thread or line

Nylon beading thread

Silk cord

Fabric and ribbon

Even though you may be a beader, you might not be a seamstress. But most wedding wearables require some sort of fabric or ribbon. Here is a list of those mentioned in the book.

Brocade. This heavy fabric features a raised design and is made of cotton, silk, or wool.

Organza. Organza is a shimmering, transparent nylon, rayon, or silk fabric that holds its shape.

Satin. This is a smooth, glossy fabric made with silk or rayon. Satin is shiny on one side, and matte on the other side.

Silk. Silkworms secrete a fiber, and people make silk fabric with it! The result is a soft, smooth, draping fabric.

Tulle. Tulle is a delicate netted fabric made out of nylon, silk, or rayon. It holds its shape and is popularly recognizable in ballet tutus.

Glue

When making some of your wedding projects, you'll find you want to work quickly to meet the big deadline. Glue is the ticket! The fastest-drying glues are the best bet for speed, but, since it's possible that the projects that require it will undergo wear and tear, you'll want to use the strongest as well. Glue as neatly as possible, but if you've got oozing here or there on a piece you might not use again after the party, don't sweat it.

For sealing knots, I recommend G-S Hypo Cement. For gluing beads to a flat surface, use E-6000 or Crafter's Goop. Use any kind of fabric glue (the glue gun kind is especially handy because it dries so fast) to attach beads to fabric. Keep that glue gun out and use multipurpose glue sticks for making attachments that don't need to be terribly strong or pretty. Terrifically Tacky Tape works great for adhering beads to vertical or oddly shaped pieces—just coat with a sealant (like Mod Podge) to secure it once it's dried.

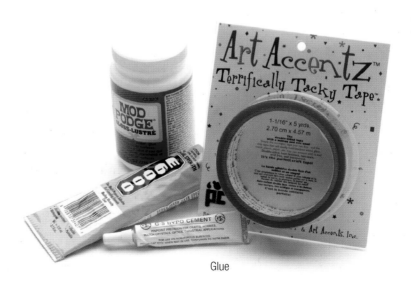

Glue

Tools

"Your beaded projects are only as good as the tools you use." A teacher told me that once. For the simple projects in this book, however, super-high-quality tools aren't necessary. But knowing which tool is which and when to use them is crucial.

Beading needles

This very thin type of needle's eye is the same width as the rest of the needle. They come in sizes #10, #12, #13, #15, and #16, with #10 being largest. They work well for very small-holed beads like small seed beads, pearls, and some semiprecious stones.

Twisted wire needles

These needles are made up of a piece of thin twisted wire with a loop at one end. You place the thread through the loop, and when you pass the needle through a bead, the loop collapses on the thread.

Chain-nose pliers

This tool has flat, tight jaws that taper to a point. It's used for gripping and bending wire.

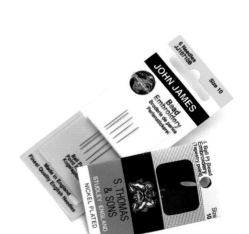

Chain-nose pliers

Crimping pliers

This specialty pliers is designed for squeezing and securing crimp tubes onto beading wire. See the next page for instructions on how to crimp.

Crimping pliers

Twisted wire needles

Beading needles

Round-nose pliers

These pliers have tapered cylindrical jaws used to make curves and loops.

Round-nose pliers

Jeweler's wire cutters

These cutters have very sharp, pointed jaws that cut beading wire, head pins, eye pins, and other soft wire.

Jeweler's wire cutters

Heavy-duty wire cutters

This type of cutters is meant for cutting very hard wire or those that are thicker than 20-gauge.

Techniques

You don't need to be a beading expert to make the projects in this book. Most of the techniques are very simple and straightforward. And for those techniques that take a little more finessing, just spend some extra time practicing to get them just right.

Working with Wire and Findings

Crimping. Crimping is the best way to secure beading wire to a clasp or other connector. To start, begin the strand of beads with a crimp tube. Pass through the clasp or connector. Pass back through the crimp tube. Snug the crimp tube and beads close to the closure. Spread the two wires so they line each side of the tube. Use the first notch on the crimping pliers (round on one jaw, dipped on the other) to squeeze the crimp tube shut. Use the second notch on the crimping pliers (rounded on both jaws) to shape the tube into a tight round. Make gentle squeezes around the tube for a perfect cylinder. Trim the tail wire close to the beads (Figures 1 and 2).

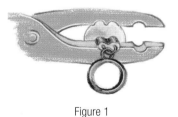

Figure 1

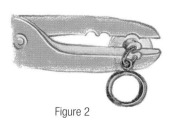

Figure 2

11

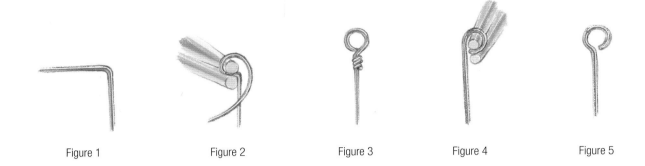

Figure 1   Figure 2   Figure 3   Figure 4   Figure 5

Looping wire. You'll need to know how to make a wire loop to make just about any beaded piece that includes wire dangles. To begin a simple loop, use chain-nose pliers to make a 90° bend ⅜" from the end of the wire. Grasp the wire end with round-nose pliers. Holding onto the wire with one hand, gently turn the pliers until the wire end and wire body touch where you made the initial bend. To make a wrapped loop, use chain-nose pliers to make a 90° bend in the wire 2" (5 cm) from one end (Figure 1). Use round-nose pliers to hold the wire near the angle and bend the short end up and around the pliers until the wire meets itself (Figure 2). Wrap the end tightly down the neck of the wire to create a couple of coils. Trim the excess close to the coils (Figure 3).

Wire Spiral. To make a decorative wire spiral, make a small loop at the end of a wire with round-nose pliers (Figures 4 and 5). Continue the spiral by holding on to the initial loop with chain-nose pliers and pushing the wire over it with your thumb (Figure 6).

Twisting wire. This technique is used quite extensively in this book. To achieve the most professional results, follow these instructions. It's also best to practice the technique before you start your project. Craft wire is fairly inexpensive, so don't hesitate to use some up before you start—it's worse to have a poor-looking piece than to use a little extra wire.

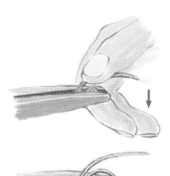

Figure 6

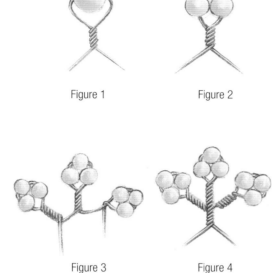

Figure 1   Figure 2

Figure 3   Figure 4

Tips

🌀 It's easiest to work this technique if you use shorter lengths of wire rather than longer. Two feet is a good length to use when making tiaras and combs. When you reach the end of a piece of wire, add a new piece by wrapping wire over the end of the previous wire, around the headband or comb base a few times, and then continue on with the pattern.

🌀 To place a bead, slide it along the wire roughly where you'd like it put, and twist the wires. You will only lose a minimum length with the twists.

🌀 Use needle-nose pliers to pull your wire through hard-to-reach places when you're twisting wire.

Note

🌀 The project instructions will assume that you know the following techniques by name. Turn back to this section for reference.

To create a simple stem, cut a piece of wire about two and a half times longer than your desired stem length. String a bead and slide it to the center of the wire. Cross the wire ends so they intersect directly below the top of the bead. Hold tightly onto the bead while you twist wires together for ½–1", one rotation at a time. Always keep the wires in a wide V-shape. The twisted stem should look like a rope, not a spiral staircase (Figure 1).

To twist a leaf stem, string 3 or more beads, cross the wires so they intersect and the beads make a loop, and twist as described above (Figure 2).

To make a three-branch stem, cut a length of wire six and a half times longer than your desired stem length. String 1 or more beads on the wire, slide them to the center of the wire, and make three to six twists. Use one wire end to string 1 or more beads and slide them just above the point you want your branch length to be. Loop the beads and twist the wire until it reaches the initial twists. Make another branch with the other wire end. Twist the two wire ends together to create the final stem (Figures 3 and 4).

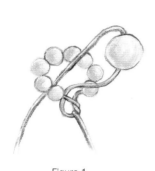

Figure 1

Figure 2

Figure 3

Figure 4

Figure 5

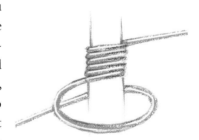

Figure 6

To make a simple flower, work it as the leaf stem, but just make one or two twists under the beads. Use one of the wire ends to pass under and up through the loop of beads. String a bead that will make the flower center and pass the wire down through the loop of beads. Cross the wires and twist the stem (Figures 1 and 2).

To begin a twisted petal flower (five petals), determine the number of beads that, once strung, will make up one petal's length. Double that number. This will be the amount of beads you'll string for each petal. Measure the length of the petal and multiply that by twelve times. Cut a length of wire to that measurement. String the predetermined amount beads on the wire and stop just slightly above the point you want your stem to begin. Split the beads in half and fold the wire so that an even number of beads are on each side of the fold. Make one or two twists right below the beads to secure them. Repeat, tightly twisting the base of each petal onto the base of the previous one. End by twisting the first and last petal bases together one or two times. Use one of the wire ends to pass under and up through the center of the flower. String a bead that will make the flower center, and pass the wire down through the loop of beads. Cross the wires and twist the stem (Figures 3, 4, and 5).

Wrapping wire. Wrapping wire is the way you secure the end of a wire to a metal base, hide twists along a base, or use as a design element by itself. When you wrap wire around something like a bobby pin or headband, make the wraps tight and close together so they resemble coils. Keep the wraps neat and trim the wire so it can't be easily seen (Figure 6).

Figure 1
Backstitch (also known as return
stitch and running stitch)

Working with Needle and Thread

Bead embroidery. Bead embroidery is a great technique to use for embellishing a dress or adding beads to a veil. Follow the illustrations below to discover how to make those embellishments used in this book. Bead embroidery is started by threading a needle with a length of beading thread that has a knot in the end. Pass through the fabric from wrong to right side so the knot catches the thread from going through. See Figures 1 through 7.

Figure 2
Chain stitch

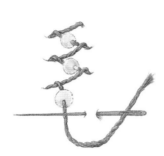

Figure 3
Cretan stitch

Figure 4
Feather stitch

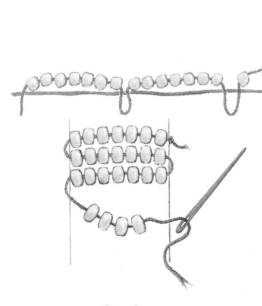

Figure 5
Fly stitch

Figure 6
Lazy stitch

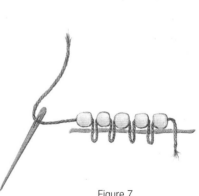

Figure 7
Single stitch

Loomwork. This technique is used to make a flat fabric of beads and thread. First, warp your loom according to the manufacturer's directions. Using a long beading needle and a 3' length of thread, string the number of beads needed for the first row. Bring the beaded thread (the weft) under the warp threads and push the beads up with your finger so there is one bead between each two warp threads. Hold the beads in place and pass back through all the beads, making sure that this time the weft thread passes over the warp threads. Repeat these steps for each row (Figure 1).

Simple fringe. Adding fringe to a sewn or beaded piece can be done in a variety of ways. The simplest way begins by anchoring a thread in the fabric or beadwork base. String a length of beads plus one bead. Skipping the last bead, pass back through all the beads just strung to create a fringe leg. Pass back into the foundation row or fabric and repeat as desired (Figure 2).

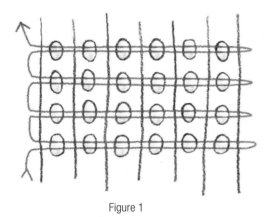

Figure 1

Figure 2

Knots

Lark's head knot. Lark's head knots are great for securing stringing material to a cord or bar. Begin by folding the stringing material in half. Bend the fold over the bar (Figure 1). Pull the ends through the loop created in Step 2 and tighten (Figure 2).

Overhand knot. This knot is the basic one for tying off thread. It is not very secure, so be careful where you use it. First make a loop with the stringing material. Pass the cord that lies behind the loop over the front cord and through the loop. Pull tight (Figure 3).

Square knot. This is the classic knot for securing most stringing materials. First make an overhand knot, passing the right end over the left end. Next, make another overhand knot, this time passing the left end over the right end. Pull tight (Figure 4).

Figure 1

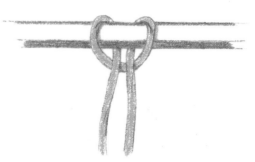

Figure 2

Figure 3

Figure 4

*A*dding beads to your invitations and thank-you notes makes them even more special and will ensure that they won't go unnoticed! You can mix up these ideas in any fashion—make an invitation using a thank-you note idea or vice versa. The instructions below give a general overview of how these particular cards were made, but you'll want to personalize those you create to make them completely your own.

Simply Sophisticated
Wedding Invitation

All cards and albums were
designed and created by
Jodi Reeb-Myers.

Materials and Tools

White ¼" organza ribbon (about 18" per invitation)

White cardstock (8½" × 5½", folds to 5½" × 4¼")

Clear shrink plastic

"You're Invited" inking stamp

Permanent black ink

¼" hole punch

Hole punch for the outline of the charm

Oven

Various white seed beads

26 mm silver craft wire

Scissors

Step 1: Fold a card using the white card-stock.

Step 2: Tie the ribbon around the card, ending with a bow. Set aside.

Step 3: Cut the charm shape out of the shrink plastic.

Step 4: Use permanent ink to stamp the shrink plastic and punch a ¼" hole at the top.

Step 5: Heat the shrink plastic in the oven according to manufacturer's directions.

Step 6: Use the wire to string the shrink plastic charm and seed beads.

Step 7: Bend the wire around the bow.

Words from the Wedding Planner

If you're doing handmade invitations and/or thank-you notes, make them well ahead of schedule and ask a friend or two for help or, trust me, they'll never get to the mailbox on time.

Quick & Easy Idea

☙ Fill your invitation's envelope with a pinch or strand of rice-shaped fresh-water pearls.

Shaker Aesthete Wedding Invitation

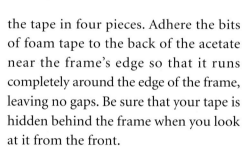

Materials and Tools

Script inking stamp	Acetate
Tan ink	3/16" double-sided tape
Cream cardstock	3/16" foam tape
(4¼" × 11" folds to	White rice
4¼" × 5½")	Various seed beads
Wedding bell inking	"You're Invited" inking
stamp	stamp
Eggplant ink	Vellum
1¼" square hole	Heat gun
punch	1/16" round hole punch
Decorative green	Vintage copper brads
paper	Lavender sheer ribbon
Scalloped scissors	Scissors

Step 1: Fold a card using the cream cardstock. Set aside.

Step 2: Stamp the background script on the cream cardstock with tan ink so it covers the entire front of the card. Let dry.

Step 3: Stamp the wedding bell on the cream cardstock in eggplant ink so the space above it is the same measurement as the spaces on each side (centered and slightly toward the top). Let dry and set aside.

Step 4: Use the square hole punch to cut a 1¼" square in the middle of the green paper. Measure about ¾" out from each side of the square you just punched, and use the scalloped scissors to trim the paper so the green paper looks like a frame.

Step 5: Adhere small pieces of the double-sided tape to the back of the paper frame and stick the front of the acetate to the tape.

Step 6: Cut a 5½" piece of foam tape and peel off the protective paper on one side. Cut the tape in four pieces. Adhere the bits of foam tape to the back of the acetate near the frame's edge so that it runs completely around the edge of the frame, leaving no gaps. Be sure that your tape is hidden behind the frame when you look at it from the front.

Step 7: With the front of the frame face down, fill the foam tape well with white rice and colored seed beads.

Step 8: Peel off the protective paper on the other side of the tape. Lay the card on top of the foam tape so that the wedding bells are framed.

Step 9: Stamp "You're Invited" on the vellum and heat-set.

Step 10: Tear the vellum above and below the stamped area.

Step 11: Punch 1/16" holes in the vellum on either side of the stamped area. Use the brads to attach the vellum to the front of the card.

Step 12: Tie the ribbon at the fold.

Pearl Band-It Wedding Invitation

Materials and Tools

Cream cardstock (4¼" × 11"
   folds to 4¼" × 5½")
Decorative paper
Ornamental inking stamp
Mossy green satin ribbon
   (about 12" per invitation)
Tiny pearl strand (about 3½" per invitation)
Scissors

Step 1: Fold a card using the cream cardstock. Set aside.

Step 2: Attach decorative paper to the front of the card leaving a border.

Step 3: Stamp the ornamental pattern on a 1¾" cardstock strip, edging with decorative scissors.

Step 4: Fold and glue the band to fit over the invitation, so it can slide easily.

Step 5: Tie the satin ribbon in a knot, threading the pearl string through the knot as you tighten it.

Step 6: Glue the ribbon to the band.

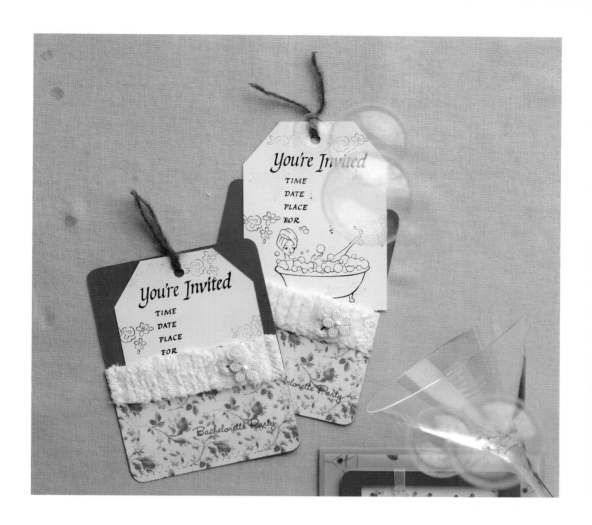

Good Girl Bachelorette Party Invitation

Materials and Tools

Decorative paper (about 4¼" × 3")

Rose cardstock (about 4¼" × 5½")

Cream cardstock tag (about 3½" × 4½")

Vintage buttons

Chenille fabric remnant

Yarn

"You're Invited," "Bachelorette Party,"
   girl in a bathtub, and flower inking stamps

Black and rose stamping inks

1.4" hole punch

Sewing thread, machine

Scissors

Step 1: Sew vintage buttons on the chenille fabric strip (about 4¼" × 1⅛").

Step 2: Layer the decorative paper and chenille fabric and sew them to the rose cardstock to create a pocket for the invitation.

Step 3: Stamp "You're Invited" in black on the tag. Stamp flowers on the tag.

Step 4: Stamp "Bachelorette Party" on the decorative paper near the bottom of the pocket.

Step 5: Punch a hole at the top of the tag and use yarn and a lark's head knot (see page 17) to make a pull.

Not-So-Good-Girl Bachelorette Party Invitation

Materials and Tools

Moss green cardstock (5½" × 8½", folds to 5½" × 4¼")

Rose and cream cardstocks

Martini vellum

Organza ribbon (about 7" for each invitation)

Various seed and bugle beads

Beverage and "Bachelorette Party" stamps

Black ink

Colored pencils

Clear acetate

Foam tape

Double-sided tape

Scissors

Step 1: Fold a card using the green cardstock.

Step 2: Attach the martini vellum to the front of the card.

Step 3: Stamp the beverage in black ink on the cream cardstock and color with colored pencils.

Step 4: Create the shaker. Begin by cutting the rose cardstock so that it makes a frame that will fit the beverage image. Follow the "Shaker Aesthete" instructions on how to make the rest of the shaker (see page 21). Fill with various beads and attach the cream stamped background. Trim the paper so none of the cream cardstock shows.

Step 5: Wrap the shaker with the sheer ribbon.

Step 6: Use the double-sided tape to adhere the shaker to the card.

Step 7: Stamp "Bachelorette Party" near the bottom of the card in black ink.

Ribboned Rehearsal Dinner Invitation

Materials and Tools
- Small sequins (about 5mm)
- Decorative papers
- Cream cardstock (5½" × 8½", folds to 5½" × 4¼")
- Satin ribbon (about 5¼" per invitation)
- PVA glue
- "You're Invited" inking stamp
- Scissors

Step 1: Fold a card using the cream cardstock.

Step 2: Adhere decorative papers to the front of the card.

Step 3: Glue sequins to the satin ribbon and glue the ribbon to the card.

Step 4: Stamp "You're Invited" on the cream cardstock and glue it to the card.

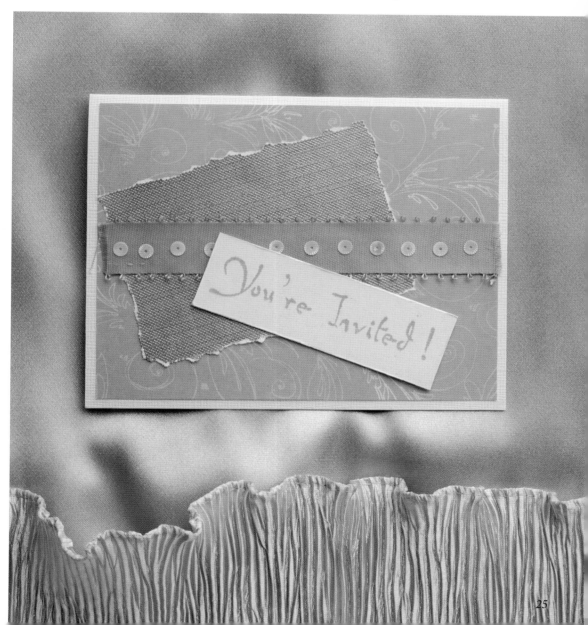

Sew Pretty Bridal Shower Invitation

Materials and Tools

White cardstock (2 pieces 6½" × 5")
Copper brads
Beaded ribbon (about 5" per invitation)
Stickers
Satin hanger sticker
Sewing pattern paper
Creamy Carmel and black inks
Wedding dress and "You're Invited" inking stamps
Vellum
Double-sided tape
Foam tape
Scissors

Step 1: Adhere the pattern paper to white cardstock. Set aside.

Step 2: Stamp the dress in black ink on white cardstock and cut it out. Place a few pieces of foam tape on the back and stick it to the pattern paper.

Step 3: Place the hanger sticker over the dress so it looks like it's hanging.

Step 4: Sew beaded ribbon to the card and embellish the paper with stickers.

Step 5: Stamp "You're Invited" on the vellum, cut it out, and adhere it to the card.

Step 6: Ink the edges of the card with the ink pad.

Step 7: Bind the card with a cardstock backing using vintage brads.

Garden Bridal Shower Invitation

Materials and Tools

Cream cardstock (4¼" × 9¾")
Decorative paper
Pearl, fire-polished, and crystal beads
Precious Metal Clay bead
Vintage pewter brads
26-gauge silver wire
Vellum
Scissors

Step 1: Use your computer to print the shower information on the vellum.

Step 2: Layer the printed vellum, decorative paper, and vanilla cardstock. Connect the three layers together with brads.

Step 3: String a random assortment of beads on the wire and attach the strand to the card by wrapping the wire around the brads.

Bridal Shower
For

Melissa

Sunday, January 23
1:30 p.m.

at Jodi's house

R.S.V.P by January 16

theme: shabby chic

You're Invited

Sew Pretty Bridal Shower Invitation

Garden Wedding Shower

For

Cindy Bride

Saturday, October 6th
3:30 p.m.

Her Mother's garden
Weddingville, USA

Please R.S.V.P
By October 3

Blushing Bridal Shower Thank-You Note

Materials and Tools

Cream cardstock (11 × 4¼", folds to 5½" × 4¼")
Moss green cardstock
Bride inking stamp
Olive ink
Colored pencils
Foam green ribbon (about 10½" per invitation)
Iridescent seed beads
Scrappy Glue

Step 1: Make a card out of the cream cardstock. Set aside.
Step 2: Stamp the image on cream cardstock and color with the colored pencils.
Step 3: Mat the stamped cream cardstock with the green cardstock.
Step 4: Glue seed beads to the dress detail.
Step 5: Tie the ribbon around the card.

Daisy Thank-You Note

Materials and Tools

Decorative papers
Light green cardstock, (8½" × 5½", folds to 4¼" × 5½")
Moss green cardstock
Paper Daisy
Light blue seed beads
Scrappy Glue
Celery grosgrain ribbon
Deckled and regular scissors

Step 1: Fold a card using the light green cardstock.
Step 2: Layer decorative paper bands onto the front of the card.
Step 3: Glue the ribbon to the band.
Step 4: Use the deckled scissors and moss cardstock to cut leaves.
Step 5: Glue the paper flower onto the band, the leaves tucked behind, and seed beads in the flower center.

Microstrip Thank-You Note

Materials and Tools

Cream cardstock 8½" × 5½" (folds to 4¼" × 5½")
Brocade blue and olive cardstock
Olive, eggplant, and brocade blue inking markers
Flower inking stamp
Sheer ribbon (about 8" per invitation)
Double-sided tape
Silver microbeads or small seed beads
5½" Terrifically Tacky Tape
Awl
Scissors

Step 1: Make a card using cream cardstock and set aside.
Step 2: Ink the stamps with markers and mist the stamp so it creates a watercolor effect when you stamp it.
Step 3: Stamp the flowers on the cream cardstock and layer it with the blue and green cardstock, adhering each layer to the next one.
Step 4: Tie the layers with a sheer ribbon and adhere all to the card.
Step 5: Adhere a strip of Terrifically Tacky Tape as a border and sprinkle with microbeads.

Blushing Bridal Shower Thank-You Note

Daisy Thank-You Note

Microstrip Thank-You Note

Whether you're hosting 15 or 150 at your wedding reception, you'll want to wow your guests with a sensational-looking table and a breath-taking wedding cake! Set a stage for memories by including some of these unique projects.

Large and Minnie Pearl Topiaries

This very simple centerpiece idea is like a chameleon. Make the prim and precious version shown here, or change the bead, flowerpot, or topiary type to suit the mood of your celebration.

Materials and Tools

2 strands of round 8mm ivory glass pearl beads
Straight pins with large, flat heads
1' foam topiary with mossy surface
Spanish moss
Terra-cotta flowerpot the same size as
   the bottom of the topiary
Paint
G-S Hypo Cement
Glue gun and glue sticks
Brush
Knife

Step 1: Use the brush to paint the pot. Let dry.

Step 2: If necessary, use the knife to trim the bottom of the topiary so it fits snugly into the pot.

Step 3: String a pearl on a pin and stick it into the topiary. Repeat all around the topiary in an even pattern until you've added all the beads. If some of the pearl holes are too big for the pins and the pearls are falling off, use a small bit of glue or Hypo Cement inside the hole to adhere the pearl to the pin.

Step 4: Set the topiary into the pot and glue the Spanish moss to the flat area of the topiary.

Materials and Tools for the place card holder

10 round 8mm ivory glass pearl beads
24-gauge dark green craft wire
Spanish moss
2" terra-cotta flowerpot
Enough modeling clay or florist foam to fill pot
Paint
Glue gun and glue sticks
Brush
Wire cutters

Step 1: Use the brush to paint the pot. Let dry.

Step 2: Cut a 3' length of wire. String 1 pearl and slide it to the middle of the wire. Twist a 2" simple stem (see page 13). String 1 pearl on one of the wire ends and twist a 1½" simple stem. Repeat on the other wire end. Continue stringing pearls and twisting simple stems. Each stem should be smaller than the last one. When you run out of pearls, twist the wire ends together for 1½", trim any excess wire, and set aside (Figure 1).

Step 3: Press the clay into the pot so it is level with the top. Stick the twisted stem into the clay at the center of the pot. Glue the moss to the top of the clay.

Step 4: Shape the twisted branches to make a pleasing arrangement.

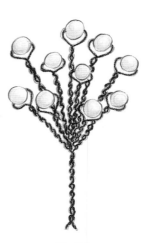

Figure 1

Thank you for
sharing in our joy!
John and Molly
2006

Maggie and Jim Bassett

Candle Splash Candleholder

Materials and Tools

132 round 4mm light green AB Czech fire-polished beads

12 round 6mm light green AB Czech fire-polished beads

20 round 8mm opaque metallic silver Czech fire-polished beads

Size 11° light green seed beads

Crystal silver-lined bugle beads

18-gauge silver craft wire

26-gauge silver craft wire

Bottle cap, ¾" deep × 1¾" wide

Silver spray paint

Tapered candle

Glue gun and glue sticks

Needle-nose pliers

Wire cutters

The water-splashed appearance of this candleholder makes it look like your candle is taking a dive!

Step 1: Make a base circle with the 18-gauge wire that will fit on the rim of the bottle cap. The ends of the wire should overlap a bit. Use 26-gauge wire to wrap the ends together (see page 14), securing the circle.

Step 2: Secure a length of 26-gauge wire to the base circle. String seven 4mm beads and 1 seed bead. Pass back through the last fire-polished strung and pull tight so the beads snug against the base circle. String four 4mm beads and pass back through the second and first beads strung in this step. Pull tight and wrap the wire around the base circle for about ¼" (see page 14).

Step 3: String 7 bugle beads, one 6mm, and 1 seed bead. Pass back through the 6mm and all of the bugle beads. Pull tight and wrap the wire around the base circle for about ¼" (Figure 1).

Figure 1

Figure 2

Step 4: Repeat Steps 2 and 3 all around the circle until you have twelve 4mm leaf shapes and twelve 6mm bugle bead sprays.

Step 5: Tightly wrap wire around the base circle to hide the wraps made to secure the beads (Figure 2).

Step 6: Use the 26-gauge wire to string all of the 8mm beads. Test to see that the strand fits snugly around the bottle cap. Make adjustments as necessary, twist the end wires to make a tight loop, and trim. Set aside.

Step 7: Spray the bottle cap, inside and out, with the spray paint. Let dry thoroughly.

Step 8: Place the bottle cap on your work surface topside down. Use the glue gun and sticks to adhere the base circle to the bottle cap's rim. Let dry. Place the 8mm bead ring around the bottle cap and slide it up against the rim. Glue it in place to hide the base circle and let dry. Glue the candle to the inside center of the bottle cap and let dry. Run a line of glue between the candlestick and the sides of the bottle cap and add the remaining 4mm beads there to hide the inside of the bottle cap. Let dry.

Little Splash Place Card

Put this place card on the same table you've set your Candle Splash Candleholder, and you'll make an even bigger splash!

Materials and Tools

10 round 6mm light green AB Czech fire-polished beads

11 round 4mm light green AB Czech fire-polished beads

26-gauge silver craft wire

Crystal silver-lined bugle beads

Size 11° light green seed beads

Place card

Tape

Wire cutters

Awl

Step 1: Cut an 18" length of wire. String seven 4mm beads and 1 seed bead, leaving a 4" tail. Pass back through the last 4mm bead strung and pull tight. String four 4mm and pass back through the second and first beads strung in this step. Twist the wire twice to secure the beads (see page 13).

Step 2: Use one wire end to string 6 bugle beads, one 6mm, and 1 seed bead. Pass back through the 6mm and all of the bugle beads. Pull tight. Repeat four times, adding stems that vary in length and variety of beads. Finish the spray by twisting the wires together several times, but don't cut the wire.

Step 3: Use the awl to poke a hole in the upper left corner of your place card. Put the wire ends through the hole and tape them to the back of the card. Trim excess wire if necessary.

Crystal Rain Vase

This vase will look stunning on a wedding dinner table. It works up quickly, and you won't break the bank—even if you have to make a dozen. Choose a flat-sided vase, and your job will be even easier.

Materials and Tools
1 large bag of clear round faceted 8mm plastic beads
Crafter's Goop or E-6000
Glass vase with 3 flat sides
Small piece of cardboard
Bubble wrap or other packing material

Step 1: Place the packing material on the work surface and lay the vase on its side on top of it. The packing material should hold the vase in place so it won't roll.

Step 2: Use the cardboard to spread a $\frac{1}{16}$" layer of glue over half of one side of the vase.

Step 3: Pour the beads on top of the glue. Make sure there are no holes between the beads.

Step 4: Dab glue on individual beads and adhere them to the side of the vase. Place the beads so they look as though they are falling into the rest of the beads (fewer at the top of the vase, more toward the middle). Let dry.

Step 5: Turn the vase and glue beads to the side the same way you did before. Let dry for a few hours, turn the vase again, glue beads, and let completely dry.

Words from the Wedding Planner

Be sure your table gifts look like a significant part of the place setting, not just a second thought. They'll seem more important if you incorporate them into the napkin placement, set them on chairs, or showcase them inside wine glasses.

Luminescent Luminaries

Embellishing a plain votive holder with seed beads is a snap to do, and the result is luminary.

Materials and Tools

3 strands of seed beads
  (still on the hank)
¾"-wide Terrifically Tacky Tape
Glass votive holder
Transparent tape
Scissors
Mod Podge
Small craft brush

Step 1: Wrap the holder with the tape in a continuous round, with no gaps in the tape. Trim. Peel the protective coating off the tape. Set the holder aside.

Step 2: Undo one end of one strand of seed beads from the hank but keep the beads on the thread. Tape the thread end with transparent tape. Hold onto the end of the thread as you wrap the beads around the votive holder, completely covering the tape. Make the wraps tight and close together. Since the beads are still on the thread, it's possible for you to pull up the beads if you make a mistake. When the strand runs out, add another, butting the first bead of the new strand up against the last bead of the old one.

Step 3: Press the beads tightly into the Tacky Tape. Trim any loose threads. Let the tape cure for 24 hours.

Step 4: Lightly cover the beads with a coat of Mod Podge and let dry.

Nifty Napkin Rings

String any type of beads onto a few coils of memory wire and you've got an instant napkin ring. Just secure the beads by using flat-nose pliers to make a bend in each end of the wire.

Quick & Easy Ideas

⊛ Sprinkle beads on the table and place a large clear plate face down over them (you don't want beads in your food!). Place a vase of flowers on top of the plate.

⊛ Glue heart beads to hat pins and stick them in the sides and top of the cake. Once you've cut into the cake, give the pins to your guests as favors.

Bubbly Glass Garlands

Use these pretty flower garlands to beautify and personalize glass stemware.

Materials and Tools
- 11 leaf-shaped dark green iridescent Czech pressed-glass beads
- 1 rose quartz button, shaped like a rose
- 22-gauge green craft wire
- Wire cutters

1. Cut a 1' length of wire. String the flower button and slide it to 1" from the end of the wire. Make several twists to secure it. String 1 leaf bead and slide it to 2" from the flower button. Make several twists to secure the wire.
2. Continue down the wire, adding leaf beads and twisting them into place, until you have used up all the beads. Trim the wire close to the last twist.

Charming Table Favors   Cheery Chair Bow

Adding a little metal charm to each of your table favors makes them even more precious. Simply thread a ribbon through the charm, and tie it around your little gift. Some wedding favor ideas: tiny bottles of wine or bubbles, sachets, pens, birdseed throws, and lollipops.

Decorating the wedding banquet doesn't need to stop at the tables' edges. Why not tie a tulle bow around each chair? For this chair bow, I've simply machine-stitched a commercial beaded fringe to a 17" × 72" piece of tulle.

Panache Cake Topper

Jamie Hogsett

This lively spray of seed beads will lend your cake top an explosion of style.

Materials and Tools

3 g peach size 11° seed beads

5 g each size 11° seed beads in yellow, mauve, lavender, rose, and golden rose

10 g green size 11° seed beads

75 mauve 4mm fire-polished beads

75 matte mauve 4mm fire-polished beads

3 sterling silver 4×4mm crimp tubes

18 yd of 26-gauge non-tarnish silver wire

Wire cutters

Nylon-jaw pliers

Flat-nose pliers

Round-nose pliers

Bead stops (alligator clips or Bead Stoppers)

Chopstick

Mighty crimping pliers

Step 1: *Leaves.* Cut a 26" piece of wire. String 1 green seed bead to the center of the wire and twist (see page 13). String 6" of green seed beads on to each end of wire. Snug the beads and place a bead stop on each wire. Use a chopstick as a form to twist the green seed beads around to form a spiral leaf.

Step 2: *Branches.* Cut a 12" piece of wire. String 1 mauve fire-polished bead 2" onto the wire and form a wrapped loop around the bead (see page 13). Keep the wrapped loop loose enough so that other fire-polished beads will slide over and cover the coil. String 24 mauve fire-pol-ished beads. Snug the beads and place a bead stop on the wire. Repeat entire step using matte mauve fire-polished beads.

Step 3: *Coils:* Cut a 20" piece of wire. String 1 yellow seed bead 2" onto the wire and form a wrapped loop around the bead. String 7–8" of yellow seed beads. Snug the beads and place bead stop on the wire. Repeat entire step for the mauve, lavender, rose, and golden rose seed beads. Make a loose coil with each tendril of beads.

Step 4: Pass the ends of all wires through one 4×4mm crimp tube. Remove all bead stops and snug the crimp tube up to all the beads. Crimp the tube.

Step 5: *Cherry blossoms:* Cut a 25" piece of wire. String 3 peach seed beads 2" onto the wire and form a wrapped loop around them. *String 3 peach seed beads ½" from the last twist of beads and twist to form a tiny petal. Repeat from * twenty-six times.

Step 6: Hold the cherry blossom piece so that the last cherry blossom is even with the crimp tube. Use the excess wire from the cherry blossom to form tight even wraps around the crimp tube (see page 14). Cover the crimp tube with wraps and continue down another ⅛". Trim the excess cherry blossom wire.

Step 7: Repeat Steps 1–6 twice more for a total of three clusters.

Step 8: Group the three clusters together. Using 9' of wire, wrap the clusters together by tightly coiling wire around the three covered crimp tubes, then moving down away from the beads. Form tight coils around all of the wires for 4½". Trim the ends of all wires.

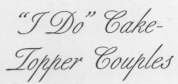

"I Do" Cake-Topper Couples

It used to be that every wedding cake had one of those ceramic bride and groom cake toppers— you know the ones! Nowadays you can think outside the box and add your own version of the classic—in beads!

Bone beads wired together and colored with permanent marker.

Printed photo with twisted wire and other bead embellishments hot-glued on.

Terrifically Tacky Taped Doll Figures.

Jitterbugging bent-wire figures with glass bead heads.

Caked with Jewelry

Oftentimes a little attention to detail is what kicks up the overall feel of an event a notch. In this case, embellish a plain pastry server with beads and wire, and make a cake stand necklace to go with it.

Materials and Tools for pastry server

Silver pastry server with slotted handle
Assorted light rose India glass beads
22-gauge silver craft wire
Flat-nose pliers
Needle-nose pliers
Round-nose pliers
Wire cutters

Step 1: Determine a spot on the server's handle from which to start and secure a wire there.

Step 2: String 1 bead and wrap the wire around the handle to seat it. String 1 or 2 more beads and wrap the handle around a different area. Continue stringing beads and wrapping until the front of the handle is completely encrusted in beads. As you work, keep your wraps tight and clean. Test the handle every so often to feel for sharp or uncomfortable areas. When you begin to run out of wire, end your wire lengths with spirals to accentuate the beads and add another design element (the large spirals take up an 8"-wire length, the small ones take 4").

Figure 1

Materials and Tools
for cake stand necklace

7 light rose 1" India glass beads
7 round 10mm light rose Czech fire-polished beads
7 round 8mm light rose Czech fire-polished beads
Size 8° ivory seed beads
Size 11° silver-lined crystal seed beads
22-gauge silver craft wire
1 silver crimp tube
Beading wire
Bead Stopper
11.25" (diameter) simple glass cake stand
Round-nose pliers
Flat-nose pliers
Needle-nose pliers
Wire cutters
Crimping pliers

Figure 2

Figure 3

Step 1: Cut one 9" piece of 22-gauge wire. Make a wrapped loop at one end (see page 12) and turn a spiral at the other (see page 12). Repeat until you have 7 large spirals in all.

Step 2: Cut one 6" piece of 22-gauge wire. Make a wrapped loop at one end and turn a spiral at the other. Repeat until you have 7 small spirals in all.

Step 3: Cut one 4" piece of 22-gauge wire. Make a simple loop at one end (see page 12). String one India glass bead and make a wrapped loop to secure the bead. Repeat until you have 7 India glass links in all.

Step 4: Cut a 1" piece of 22-gauge wire. Make a simple loop on one end. String one 10mm bead and make a simple loop to secure the bead. Repeat until you have seven 10mm links in all.

Step 5: Cut a ¾" piece of 22-gauge wire. Make a simple loop on one end. String one 8mm bead and make a simple loop to secure the bead. Repeat until you have seven 8mm links in all.

Step 6: Link together one 8mm link, one 10mm, and 1 small spiral (Figure 1). Set aside. Repeat until you have 7 short dangles in all.

Step 7: Link together 1 India glass link and 1 large spiral (Figure 2). Set aside. Repeat until you have 7 long dangles in all.

Step 8: Cut a 36" length of beading wire and put a Bead Stopper at the end. String 52 silver-lined crystals , 2 ivory seed beads, 1 short dangle, and 2 ivory seed beads. Repeat until you've used up all the short dangles. Put another Bead Stopper on the end of the strand.

Step 9: Cut a 48" length of beading wire. Put a Bead Stopper on the wire and pass the wire through the first 2 beads strung in Step 8. String 40 seed beads, 1 long dangle, and 40 seed beads. Pass through the 2 seeds beads strung before the first short dangle (on the first strand of beads), the dangle, and the 2 seed beads strung after the dangle. Repeat along the length of the first strand of beads, stringing beads and long dangles and making swags to the next short dangle.

Step 10: Pair the first and second strand wire ends. String 1 crimp tube on one end, and pass the other wire ends back through the tube (Figure 3). Crimp the tube and trim.

*F*lowers! What would a wedding be without them? You may choose to have an over-the-top designer bouquet created just for your wedding, or you may plan to simply hold a bunch of daisies gathered with a single ribbon. For either bouquet, beads are a natural addition to lend glimmer and color. But you don't need to stop at adding beads to your bouquet. You can add beads to floral cake toppers and centerpieces, groomsmen boutonnieres, and ceremony flower arrangements, as well as the fresh flowers you might plan on wearing in your hair.

Pretty Little Bouquet Additions

Arlene Baker

Delicate and airy, these diminutive beaded flowers and ferns will add just the right touch of sparkle to your special wedding accessories. Use them in your bridal bouquet, twine several pieces in your bridal headpiece, attach them to your ring bearer's pillow or wind a fern sprig and flower around a wedding favor, place card, or satin bow. Use them in table arrangements or on top of a cake. The possibilities are endless!

Lacy Fern

Materials and Tools

Size 11° seed beads
28-gauge silver craft wire
Wire cutters

Step 1: Leaving the wire on the spool, string about 8" of seed beads. Bend the end of the wire so the beads don't slide off. Don't cut the wire.

Step 2: Slide 10 beads to 2" from the end of the wire. Cross the wires and wrap the tail wire tightly (see page 13) around the beaded portion of the wire two times so the 10 beads make a tight loop. Trim the tail wire close to the wrap.

Step 3: Slide 3 more beads next to the loop you just made (Figure 1) and hold them in place while you slide 10 more beads down the wire. Use these 10 beads to make another loop as you did in Step 2, but this time secure the loop with 1 tight twist. Place this loop on the right side of the stem (Figure 2).

Step 4: Repeat Step 3 seven times, placing one loop on the left, one on the right, and so on.

Step 5: Slide 1" of beads to the bottom of the fern and temporarily hold them in place with a piece of tape. Cut the wire from the spool so there is 5" of bare wire on the base of the fern frond. Set aside.

Step 6: Repeat Steps 1 through 5. When you've completed the second fern frond, remove the tape on the first frond, put the two fronds next to each other so the stem beads at the bottom are lined up evenly. Make sure the beads are tight (it helps to turn the unit upside down and let gravity work for you). Cross one bare wire over the other, directly below the beads. Twist the two wires tightly together for about 1" (see page 13). Straighten both wires. Trim the ends evenly, leaving the untwisted portion of the wires long.

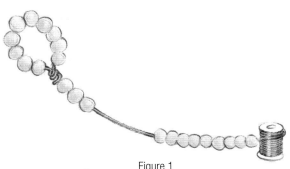

Figure 1

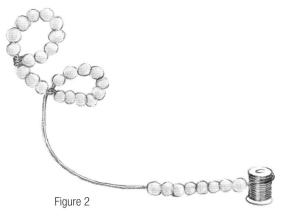

Figure 2

Forget-me-knot blossoms

Laced leaf

Baby's breath

Lacy fern

Simple stem

51

Forget-Me-Knot Blossoms

Materials and Tools

Size 11° seed beads.

28-gauge silver craft wire

Size 4mm pearl or crystal bead for flower center.

Step 1: Leaving the wire on the spool, string about 8" of seed beads. Bend the end of the wire so the beads don't slide off. Don't cut the wire.

Step 2: Slide 10 beads to 6" from the end of the wire. Cross the wires and make a twist to form a tight loop of beads (see page 13). Let 18 beads slide down the wire until they reach the twist. Loop the beads around so they hug the first loop. Swing the wire attached to the spool so it's perpendicular to the tail wire. Make one wrap (Figure 1). Don't cut the wire.

Step 3: Repeat Step 2 to make a second petal attached to the first (Figure 2). Continue repeating Step 2 until you have 5 petals in all.

Step 4: To make the blossom's center and finish the flower, slide any extra beads back toward the spool to expose a length of bare wire equal to the length of the knotted end of the wire plus about 1". Cut the wire from the spool at that measurement. Bring the petals together to form a circle. Cross one bare wire over the other directly below the beads and make two tight twists.

Step 5: String 1 pearl on the long end of the wire and let it slide toward the petals. Bring the bead and the wire up between the first and fifth petals you made. Adjust the position of the pearl so it nestles in the center of the blossom, filling the open space completely.

Hold the bead in place and keep the wire taut. Bring the long wire across the blossom, then down between the second and third petals. Bend the wire underneath the flower so it meets the short wire. Cross these two wires next to the bottom of the flower and twist 3".

Words from the Wedding Planner

If you're working with a florist, depend on their expertise for help! You make the beaded flower additions, hand them off to her, and she can add them to your bouquet.

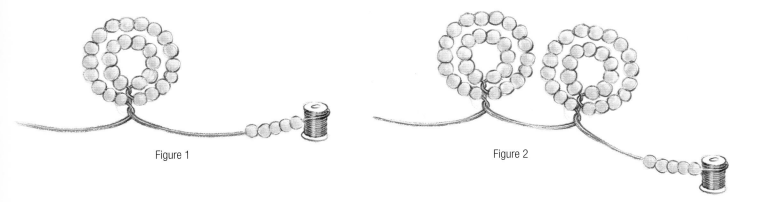

Figure 1   Figure 2

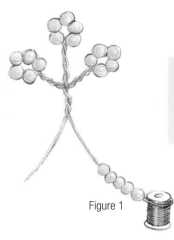

Figure 1

Figure 2

Baby's Breath

Materials and Tools
Size 11° seed beads
34-gauge silver craft wire
Wire cutters

Step 1: Leaving the wire on the spool, string about 12" of seed beads. Bend the end of the wire so the beads don't slide off. Don't cut the wire.

Step 2: Slide 5 beads to about 12" from the end of the wire. Twist the beads into a tight loop and continue twisting for about ½" (see page 13). You can keep the beads in place and make the twists smooth and tight if you hold the loop upside down and turn the loop instead of the bare wires. This is a simple stem.

Step 3: Repeat twice to make 2 simple stems that are attached to the first one (Figure 1). Change the length of the stems slightly so the flowers look more natural. Twist the spool and tail wires together for ½".

Step 4: Make another 1 or 2 simple stems and twist the spool and tail wires together for about ¾", and then make another simple stem. Twist the spool and tail wires together for 2–3" beyond the last stem and cut the spool wire (Figure 2).

Quick & Easy Idea
⚘ Use a hot glue gun to adhere pearls to the center of a flower like stephanotis.

Laced Leaf

Materials and Tools
9 round 4mm glass pearl beads
28-gauge silver craft wire
Wire cutters

Step 1: Cut one 15" length of wire. String 1 pearl and slide it to the middle of the wire. Pass one end of the wire through the pearl again and tighten (Figure 1).

Step 2: String 2 pearls on one end of the wire. Pass back through the 2 pearls with the other wire end. Pull both ends of the wire to snug the pearls, making sure there are no gaps between them. Keep the wire loops between the rows even on both sides of the pearls.

Step 3: String 3 pearls on one end of the wire, pass back through them with the other wire end, and pull tight.

Step 4: String 2 pearls on one end of the wire, pass back through them with the other wire end, and pull tight.

Step 5: String 1 pearl on one end of the wire, pass back through it with the other wire end, and pull tight. Twist the wires tightly together for 2–3" (Figure 2).

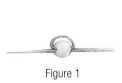

Figure 1

Figure 2

Orange Blossom

Materials and Tools

45 round 3mm glass pearl beads
1 round 4mm glass pearl or crystal bead
34-gauge silver craft wire
28-gauge silver craft wire
Wire cutters

Step 1: Follow the instructions for the Laced Leaf on page 53, but this time using 34-gauge wire and 3mm beads, and only make a ¼" (instead of 2–3") final twist. Repeat until you have 5 leaves (now petals) in all. Set aside.

Step 2: Cut a 12" length of 28-gauge wire. Make a simple stem by stringing one 4mm bead, sliding it to the middle of the wire, and twisting the wires together for ½" right under the pearl.

Step 3: To assemble the flower, put the 5 petals together, making sure the bottom beads are lined up evenly. Pass the stem you made in Step 2 through the center of the 5 petals, but don't push it to the bottom (it should extend slightly above the opening inside the flower). Hold all the pieces tightly together with one hand and use your other hand to twist all the wires tightly together for about 2". Keep the twists smooth and even and do not allow the petals to shift out of shape.

Embellished Stem Wrap

To make a wrapped bouquet even more special, use a needle and thread and spot stitch to sew pearls right onto the ribbon. Be sure you're adding the pearls in places other than where you'll be holding onto the bouquet. For an added effect, make simple fringe legs to hang off the bottom of the bouquet.

Note: If you wish to do this project but are using fresh flowers, work with your florist so you can make a ribboned sheath for your flowers to fit into on the big day.

Jaunty Boutonniere

Orange Blossom

Jaunty Boutonniere

I bet you can make this happy little everlasting boutonniere in less time than you might spend paging through a phone book to find a florist!

Materials and Tools

7 potato-shaped 6mm white freshwater pearl beads

3 faceted teardrop 10×15mm blue agate beads

24-gauge silver craft wire

1' of 4"-wide white tulle

6" of light blue organza ribbon

Wire cutters

Scissors

Step 1: Use the wire and 1 pearl to twist a 2" simple stem (see page 13). Set aside. Repeat until you have 7 pearl simple stems in all.

Step 2: Use the wire and 1 teardrop bead to twist a 2" simple stem. Set aside. Repeat twice until you have 3 teardrop simple stems in all.

Step 3: Gather the simple stems and make a pleasing arrangement, staggering the beads. Use wire to wrap the stems into position (see page 14), starting from ½" below the bead at the lowest point in the arrangement, and 1" down the twisted wires.

Step 4: Wrap the tulle around the wire you added in the previous step, covering all the stem wires. Secure the tulle by wrapping the ribbon around the stem. Finish by tying a bow that sits at the front of the boutonniere.

Fleurs de Filles Basket

A ribbon-festooned basket filled with flower petals isn't quite complete until you add a few beaded flowers on the outside!

Materials and Tools

1 spool of 26-gauge silver craft wire
15–20 bicone 6mm peridot AB Swarovski crystal beads
15–20 dark rose 6mm Czech pressed-glass flower beads
15–20 white size 11° seed beads
8' of ¾" white satin ribbon
8' of ¾" olive satin ribbon
White wicker basket
Needle-nose pliers
Wire cutters

Step 1: Cut an 18" length of wire.

Step 2: String 1 crystal and slide it 6" down the wire. Twist a ¼" simple stem (see page 13). String 1 flower bead and 1 seed bead. Pass back through the flower bead and make a ¼" stem. Repeat this step twice. Twist all of the stems together.

Step 3: Repeat Step 2 at the other end of the wire so you have one flower arrangement at each end of the wire. Wrap the little garland around the basket handle where it meets the basket. The beads should face out.

Step 4: Cut 3' of the white ribbon. Put this length and the olive ribbon together and tie a bow. Wire the bow to the basket where the garland was placed.

Step 5: Tie the remaining ribbon around the basket handle to cover the wires showing on the inside of the basket. Trim all of the ribbon lengths to your desired length.

Step 6: Repeat Steps 1 through 5 for the other side of the basket.

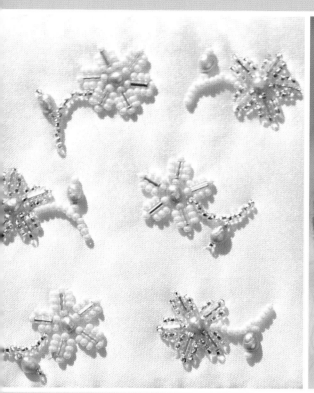

F or many brides, two of the most beautiful parts of their wedding finery are the first things they envision when preparing for the big day: a glistening gown topped off by a beautiful veil, tiara, or comb piece. You can save a lot of money by making your own wedding finery using beads. Whether you're adding beads to an existing dress or fashioning a headpiece that's as unique as you are, you're sure to impress your guests and be left with enough change to spend on your honeymoon.

Wedding Dress Embellishments

All samples were designed and crafted by Dustin Wedekind.

Your dress may be exactly the thing you were looking for—the perfect fit, fabric, and fandangles. But it may also be that the dress you bought is simply a canvas waiting to be painted with beads.

Bead embroidery on fine fabric is usually done using beading thread and beading needles.

You shouldn't need to stretch your fabric on an embroidery hoop if you're working on fabric that's already sewn into a garment. Just keep your tension even and knot your thread often in the fabric.

Materials and Tools

Seed beads
Bugle beads
Sequins
4–6mm freshwater pearls
Size B or D Nymo beading thread, color to match fabric
Beading needles
Scissors

Words from the Wedding Planner

Embellishing a dress or gown with beads should add to, not detract from, your formalwear. In other words (and in most cases) less is more!

Lines

You can work rows of beads vertically around the bodice or shape around seams as a decorative accent. Alternate line styles to create textures, such as wavy lines between straight lines (Bodice 1).

Bodice 1

Straight lines: Pass up through the fabric. String 4 beads, pass down through fabric, then pass up through fabric between the second and third beads. Pass through the last 2 beads, string 4 beads and repeat.

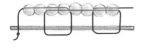

Straight lines

Dashed lines: Pass up through the fabric. String 1–4 beads, pass down through the fabric, then pass up near the last bead and repeat.

Dashed lines

Roped lines: Pass up through the fabric. String 3–4 beads, pass down through the fabric, then pass up next to the last bead and repeat.

Roped lines

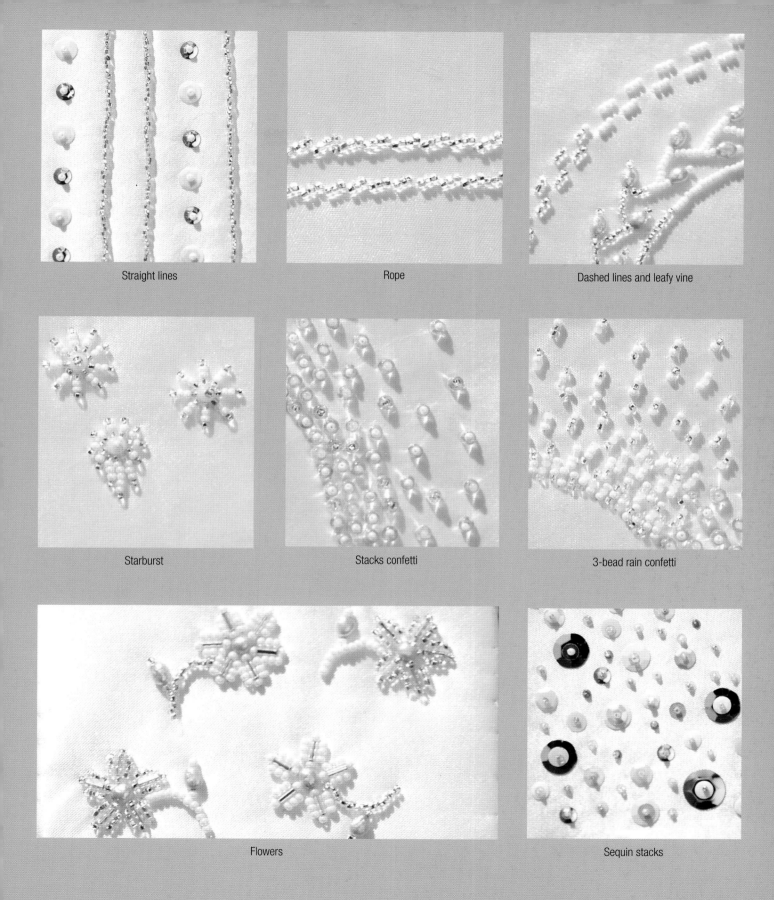

Straight lines

Rope

Dashed lines and leafy vine

Starburst

Stacks confetti

3-bead rain confetti

Flowers

Sequin stacks

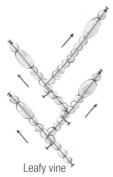

Leafy vine

Edging

Almost any traditional embroidery stitch looks good as an edging, so when you're embroidering a wedding dress, just add beads!

Leafy vine: String 8 size 11°s, 1 pearl, and 1 size 11°. Slide the beads down and pass through the fabric after the last bead, pass up through the fabric and through the fourth bead strung. String 8 size 11°s, 1 pearl, and 1 size 11°. Slide the beads down at a 30° angle to those just stitched. Pass through the fabric and repeat.

Allover Designs

Add a solo version of one of the following designs to a dress or stitch them all over to make a pattern.

Starburst: String 1 size 8° and 1 size 11°. Pass back through the size 8° and the fabric. *Pass up through the fabric next to the size 8°. String 3–5 size 11°s and pass through the fabric, radiating straight out from the size 8°. Repeat from * all around the size 8°.

Flower: Stitch 1 pearl. *Pass up through the fabric next to the pearl. String 1 size 11°, 1 bugle, and 1 size 11°. Pass down through the fabric straight out from the pearl. Repeat from * to make 5 spokes around the pearl. Pass up next to the pearl, string 3 size 11°s and pass down next to a bugle bead; repeat around to add 3 beads to each side of each bugle bead. Work a curved line of 8–12 seed beads to form a stem, and a pearl for a leaf.

Starburst

Flower

Confetti

This can be worked as allover pattern or concentrate the beads along an edge and disperse them out as you move away from the edge for a soft, shimmering highlight (Bodice 2).

3-bead rain: Work two or three rows of 3-bead stitches close to an edge, then work more rows below, spacing the stitches farther apart.

Bodice 2

Stacks: Sew sequins or size 8° seed beads close together.

Facing page, *Wedding Shawl*, by Nancy Dale

Quick & Easy Ideas

☙ Use fabric glue to adhere beads as desired.
☙ Use Terrifically Tacky Tape to secure a commercially beaded ribbon to your hem.
☙ Cut off existing spaghetti straps and add a strand of round crystal beads instead. Simply measure the old straps, string that length of beads on beading wire, crimp each end to a split or soldered ring, and sew the rings to the dress.

Grecian Headband

If you're looking for a no-frills headpiece, make this pearl-embellished headband. It looks good when you wear it like a traditional headband (over the top of the head), but you can also tip it up so it rides parallel with your eyes. It'll make you look like a Greek goddess!

Materials and Tools

Metal headband with wire teeth

1 spool of 24-gauge craft wire to match the headband

32 potato-shaped 6mm white freshwater pearl beads

Needle-nose pliers

Wire cutters

Quick & Easy Idea

❧ When you are having your hair done, have the stylist weave crystals and/or pearls through your hair.

Step 1: Secure a length of wire around one end of the base of the headband.

Step 2: String 1 pearl, wrap around the headband, around the first tooth, and back up. Continue across the headband, always keeping the direction of the wraps consistent so the pearls all lay in the same direction (Figure 1). If you need to add a new wire, begin by wrapping it around the closest tooth so the wrap doesn't show on the headband itself. Since this pattern is so simple, and the metal headband won't be hidden, you don't want any extra wire to show.

Step 3: Secure the wire by wrapping it around the band and trim.

Note

❧ When buying a metal comb, headband, or bobby pin, choose a color that not only goes well with your beads and wire, but will look good with your hair color.

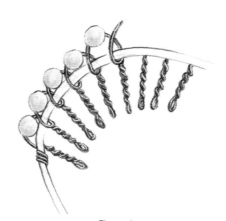

Figure 1

Karen's Comb

Nancy Dale

Nancy created this piece for the daughter of a friend. Karen looked lovely!

Materials and Tools

4½" silver metal comb with 29 wire teeth
1 spool of 26-gauge silver craft wire
100 potato-shaped 4mm ivory freshwater pearls
25 tiny ivory freshwater pearls
20 round 4mm crystal AB crystal beads
20 round 3mm crystal AB crystal beads
Ivory and crystal AB size 11° seed beads
Needle-nose pliers
Wire cutters

Step 1: Secure a length of wire around one end of the base of the comb.

Step 2: Make a series of ½–1" twisted-wire embellishments (see page 13) across the headband in a full and random pattern. Intersperse 4mm pearl 3-branch stems, 1-crystal or tiny pearl simple stems, and 3-seed-bead leaf stems (see page 13). Make the beading very full in the middle of the comb and slightly less full toward the ends. Keep the 4mm pearls toward the center of the beading and let the other small-bead stems point outward, creating small sprays here and there. The beading should be full enough so that the comb's band is completely hidden.

Step 3: Secure the wire by wrapping it around the band and trim. Shape the stems so they make a pleasing arrangement.

Aurora Borealis Comb

This elegant comb's crystals glisten and float among the substantial pearls they are nestled into. The piece looks great as a fastener for a French roll hairdo.

Materials and Tools

4½" silver metal comb with 29 wire teeth
1 spool of 24-gauge silver craft wire
38 potato-shaped 6mm white freshwater pearls
45 bicone 4mm crystal AB Swarovski crystal beads
Needle-nose pliers
Wire cutters

Step 1: Secure a 2' length of wire to the top of one of the comb's end teeth. Move the wire so it comes up along the back of the comb.

Step 2: String 1 pearl, pass the wire down in front of the comb, wrap it around the back of the first wire tooth, and pass it back up to the front of the comb (Figure 1). Repeat all across the comb to add 20 pearls in all. The pearls should sit neatly on top of the comb's metal band to hide it. Finish the wire by wrapping around the last wire tooth twice and weave up between the last 2 pearls added.

Step 3: String 1 pearl and loop the wire between the second- and third-to-the-last pearls added in Step 2 (Figure 2). Continue across, placing a pearl between two pearls from those added in Step 2.

Step 4: Make five 1-crystal ½" simple stems (see page 13) that come off of the first tooth on the comb. Wrap around the second tooth and make one 1-crystal simple stem tall enough to peek behind, up, and over the second row of pearls (Figure 3). Continue across, making 1-crystal simple stems. When you reach the end, add 5 stems as you did at the beginning of the row.

Step 5: Pass the wire up between the pearls where you made your first looped connection in Step 3. String 1 crystal and pass back down where you just exited. Pass back up so that you've looped around one of the wires placed between the first and second rows of pearls. This will seat the crystal in place between a set of 4 pearls (Figure 4). Continue across, adding 1 crystal and weaving the wire between the two rows of pearls. When finished, secure the wire and trim.

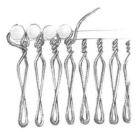

Figure 1

Figure 2

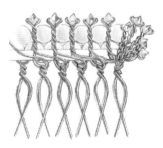

Figure 3

Figure 4

Springtime Spray Headband

Nancy Dale

This ribbon-wrapped headband is a vision for a spring wedding.

Materials and Tools

Silver metal headband with wire teeth

1 spool of 26-gauge silver craft wire

15–20 potato-shaped 4mm ivory freshwater pearls

25 tiny ivory freshwater pearls

Size 11° white seed beads

30" of ⅛"-wide white satin ribbon

Fabric glue (or needle and thread)

Needle-nose pliers

Wire cutters

Step 1: Secure a length of wire around one end of the base of the headband.

Step 2: Make a series of ½–1" twisted-wire embellishments across the headband in a loose and random pattern. Begin by working twisted petal flowers (5 petals with 8 seed beads per petal) (see page 14) across the band placed every 1½" or so. Make another pass across the band, this time interspersing 8-seed-bead leaf stems (see page 13), 3-seed-bead leaf stems (see page 13), and tiny and 4mm pearl 3-branch stems (see page 13). Keep the beading very loose and open.

Step 3: Secure the wire by wrapping it around the band and trim.

Step 4: Leaving a 2" tail of ribbon extended beyond one end, wrap the ribbon from one end of the headband to the other to hide the wire twists. Keep the ribbon flat and untwisted as it goes around and between the teeth.

Step 5: Tuck both ends of the ribbon neatly underneath each end of the headband. Finish by gluing or stitching the ribbon in place.

Fairy Queen Veil

This woodland fairy-inspired headpiece has the magical look of a butterfly whose delicate antennae are gently framing your face.

Materials and Tools

4½" plastic comb with white tulle base

1 spool of 26-gauge silver craft wire

13 round 10mm crystal AB Czech fire-polished beads

20 round 8mm crystal AB Czech fire-polished beads

30 round 6mm crystal AB Czech fire-polished beads

40 round 4mm crystal AB Czech fire-polished beads

Size 2 transparent silver-lined bugle beads

Size 11° transparent silver-lined seed beads

2 yd of white tulle

White sewing thread

5 tiny safety pins

Sewing machine

Needle-nose pliers

Wire cutters

Step 1: Fold the tulle in half. Make tiny gathers along the fold so that the tulle bunches up at this end. Make the gathers neat and consistent (Figure 1). The final width of the tulle should be 4½". Use the sewing machine and thread to sew the folds into place about ¾" from the initial fold. Set aside.

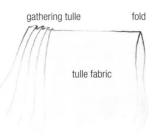

Figure 1

Step 2: *Note:* Because the comb's teeth are plastic and could be prone to breakage, avoid wrapping any wire around the teeth in the following instructions. Instead, wrap the wire around the comb's base.

Secure a length of wire that wraps around one end of the comb. String 14 bugle beads, one 10mm fire-polished bead, and 1 seed bead. Pass back through the 10mm and all the bugle beads and pull tight (Figure 2). Continue making bugle bead and fire-polished sprays at this end of the comb, one more like the one you just made; two with 12 bugle beads and one 8mm; two with 10 bugle beads and one 6mm; and two with 8 bugle beads and one 6mm. As you add the sprays, keep the longer ones toward the end of the comb, and add the smaller sprays into the first inch or so of the comb's band. Repeat for the other end of the comb.

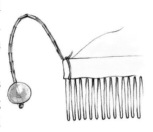

Figure 2

Figure 3

Step 3: Secure a length of wire to one end of the comb. String one 10mm and wrap the wire so that the bead covers the side of the comb band. String several 4mm and wrap the wire around the comb band near the 10mm.

Figure 4

Continue stringing beads and wrapping them around the comb band to cover the band and hide the wires added in Step 2. Keep the beads to the back (concave side) of the comb so you can attach your veil to the front side. As you make the wraps, work in a sort of freeform fashion, mixing up the bead combinations so that sometimes you string 4mms with 6mms and so on. The goal is to completely cover the comb band, so you'll need to add smaller beads to fill the holes between the larger ones. Always keep your wire hidden. As you move across the comb, gradually increase the size of beads you're using in your wraps. Once you reach the middle, you should use up six more of the 10mms. Reverse the size order when you cross to the other side, and end with a 10mm to cover the end of the band.

Step 4: Pin the right side of the veil where you sewed the gathers to the front of the comb. The veil should point up, not down (Figure 4). Let the veil drop back behind the comb as shown in the photo. Shape the beads in a pleasing arrangement.

Pearl Blossom Tiara

Spike the beads up on this tiara for a very striking, regal look, or squish them down to make an understated line of sparkle.

Materials and Tools

Silver metal headband with 37 wire teeth

1 spool of 24-gauge silver craft wire

24 round 8mm crystal AB Czech fire-polished beads (large)

18 round 6mm crystal AB Czech fire-polished beads (medium)

72 round 4mm crystal AB Czech fire-polished beads (small)

50 round 6mm lavender Swarovski pearl glass beads

Needle-nose pliers

Wire cutters

Step 1: Secure a length of wire around one end of the base of the headband.

Step 2: String 1 medium fire-polished bead, wrap around the nearest tooth and come back up. String 1 pearl, wrap around the next tooth and come back up. Repeat the sequence across the width of the headband.

Step 3: Start a new wire at the first end of the headband. String 4 small fire-polished and 1 pearl. Make a ½" twisted simple stem (see page 13) for the pearl and pass back down through the last fire-polished you just strung. String 3 more small fire-polished and wrap the wire around the headband so it straddles the medium fire-polished already placed on the headband (Figure 1). Repeat to add 8 twisted stems over the first 8 medium fire-polished placed, and add 8 more twisted stems over the last 8 medium fire-polished placed.

Step 4: Make large fire-polished bead simple stems on every other tooth of the headband. Start out with ½" stems, and increase them gradually so you reach a 2" stem length at the center.

For the immediately left-of-center stem position, add 3 individual stems. In the center stem position, make 6 individual stems. In the immediately right-of-center, make 3 individual stems. Continue across the headband, making 1 stem in each position and gradually decreasing the stem size as you move to the end.

Step 5: Make 3 simple flowers (see page 13) in the center of the tiara using pearls for petals and 1 medium fire-polished bead for the center. Make 1 simple flower with the same beads halfway between the center and the end on one side and repeat for the other side.

Step 6: Secure all wires by wrapping them tightly around the band and trim any excess wire.

Step 7: Shape the stems so they make a pleasing arrangement.

Figure 1

Parrish Crown

This crown, inspired by the fantasy illustrations of Maxfield Parrish, is designed so that even though your wedding is over, you'll still be reminded of the special day every time you wear it as a necklace!

Materials and Tools

1 spool of 24-gauge silver craft wire

Size 8° dusty rose hex seed beads

2 strands of potato-shaped 5mm light green freshwater pearl beads

2 strands of potato-shaped 6mm ivory freshwater pearl beads

12 round 6mm rose alabaster Swarovski crystal beads

20 alabaster AB starflower beads

5 alabaster AB tulip beads

22 small topaz AB leaf beads

Small sterling silver lobster clasp

Needle-nose pliers

Wire cutters

Step 1: Cut a 3' length of wire and string 10 seed beads. With the beads near the end of the wire, make a twist (see page 13) to secure them.

Step 2: String 6 green pearl beads. Twist 1 crystal bead onto the wire using 2–3 twists. Repeat eight times.

Step 3: String 3 ivory pearls and 1 crystal. Continue the strand by stringing enough ivory pearls so the strand almost fits comfortably around your head. End the strand by twisting on 1 crystal, stringing 4 ivory pearls, twisting on 1 crystal, and stringing 3 ivory pearls. Secure the lobster clasp so it is snug against the beads. Trim the excess wire.

Step 4: Secure a 3' length of wire onto the twist that lies between the seed beads and the green pearls. Make a twisted flower cluster as shown in Figure 1. To begin, string 1 starflower and 1 leaf. Pass back through the flower, make 1 twist, and wrap the wire onto the first twist. String 1 tulip and 1 seed bead, pass back through the tulip, and make 1 twist. String 14 seed beads, make a twist to form a loop, and wrap the wire between the beads on the initial strand. String 6 ivory pearls, drape them to the first crystal strung, and make a wrap around the crystal twist.

Make another twisted flower cluster that's slightly different than the first one you just made. Be sure that the cluster is firmly attached to the first pearl strand near the crystal and that the wraps and twists are as hidden as possible. String another 6 ivory pearls and drape them to the next crystal. Repeat across until you have 8 swags of ivory pearls. As you make the different flower clusters, try to create a free-form and spontaneous look by sometimes adding seed-bead loops, sometimes having the star flower sit at the top, and sometimes letting it sit at the bottom (Figure 2). Once finished making the swags, end with a flower cluster that includes 2 seed-bead loops.

Step 5: String enough seed beads to wrap around the pearl strand and stretch to the next crystal. String 1 starflower and 1 leaf. Pass back through the flower, make 1 twist, and wrap around the pearl strand next to the crystal. Repeat to reach the following crystal. Secure and trim the wire.

Step 6: Start a new wire on the last crystal strung in Step 3 and repeat Step 5 in reverse so the sides of the crown look somewhat even.

Step 7: Cut a 6" length of wire and secure it to the first flower cluster made. Make several loops behind the cluster to act as the loop for the clasp. Be sure the loop is positioned behind the cluster so that when the crown (or necklace) is worn, the clasp can't be seen. Secure the wire and trim.

Step 8: Shape the flower clusters and pearl swags so they sit in a pleasing arrangement.

Figure 1

Figure 2

Flowery Flower Girl Comb

This sweet comb is just right for a little one's special hairdo. (See the matching basket on page 57.)

(See the matching basket on page 57.)

Materials and Tools

2" silver metal comb with 12 wire teeth

1 spool of 26-gauge silver craft wire

12–15 bicone 6mm peridot AB Swarovski crystal beads

12–15 dark rose 6mm Czech pressed-glass flower beads

12–15 white seed beads

Needle-nose pliers

Wire cutters

Step 1: Secure a 2' length of wire around one end of the base of the headband.

Step 2: Make one 1-crystal ¼" simple stem (see page 13) and wrap the wire around the first tooth on the comb. String 1 flower bead and 1 seed bead. Pass back through the flower bead and make a ¼" stem. Wrap the wire around the first tooth on the comb.

Step 3: Repeat Step 2 across the comb to add 1 crystal and 1 flower to each comb tooth.

Step 4: Secure the wire by wrapping it around the comb and trim.

Step 5: Shape the beads so that they are in a pleasing arrangement and none of the comb shows when it is worn in the hair.

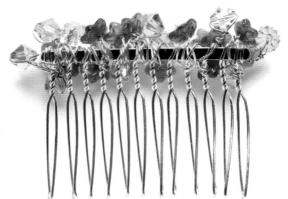

Bridal Bobbies

These pretty pins are meant to create subtle dots of color and glints of sparkle in your hair. They can be made with any type or color of beads, but you probably don't want them to get too heavy, or they'll fall right out.

All of these pins begin by using wire to make several tight wraps at the bend in the bobby pin. Next, string the beads or make a twisted wire assortment and lay it along the straight side of the pin. Add a puff of tulle if you want to add softness. Finish by making several tight wraps to stabilize the beads.

Adding a Veil to a Headpiece

Many brides would like to wear a veil at the ceremony but are happy to be rid of it once the party begins. To make a detachable veil that works with any of the following headbands or combs, you've got a variety of options. One down-and-dirty way is to simply attach tiny safety pins to the top of the veil so that you can pin the veil to the headpiece. You could also sew one side of a Velcro strip to the inside of the comb or headband and the other side of the strip to the veil. Another way is to buy a commercial braiding that has small elastic loops placed every ½". You sew the braiding to the top edge of your veil, loop-side up. Then, when you make your beaded comb, make sure you have a 4mm bead placed every ½" so you can button the loops onto the beads, attaching the veil to the comb.

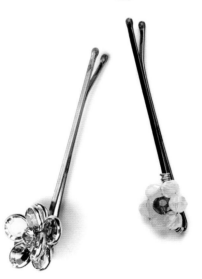

Adding Beads to a Veil

You can add beads and crystals to a purchased or handmade veil fairly easily. Just decide on how you want your pattern to look and then determine the attaching method that works best for you.

Gluing Method: Spread pieces of waxed paper on your work surface, and place the veil fabric on top of the waxed paper with the right side facing up. Make sure that the fabric lays flat on the waxed paper wherever a bead will be applied. Use a toothpick to place a small dot of clear-drying fabric glue on the veil where a bead will be located. Use tweezers to pick up a bead and set it on the dot of glue. Repeat for each bead. Care needs to be taken that the fabric is not moved until the glue has dried. Carefully peel away any waxed paper that has become stuck to back of the fabric.

Note: It is best to test gluing beads on a small swatch of the veil fabric before gluing onto a finished veil.

Sewing Method: Thread a beading needle with a short length of fine sewing thread in a color to match the veil. Pull both ends of the thread together. Make a small knot with the ends of the thread. With one hand, hold the knotted end of the thread near the inside of the veil to prevent it from pulling through to the right side. With the needle in the other hand, carefully pass through the fabric from the wrong side to right side. String a bead and pass back down through the fabric right next to the place you exited. Pass the needle through the knot and tighten the thread. Secure the thread by going in and out of the knot a couple of times. Carefully trim the thread close to the knot.

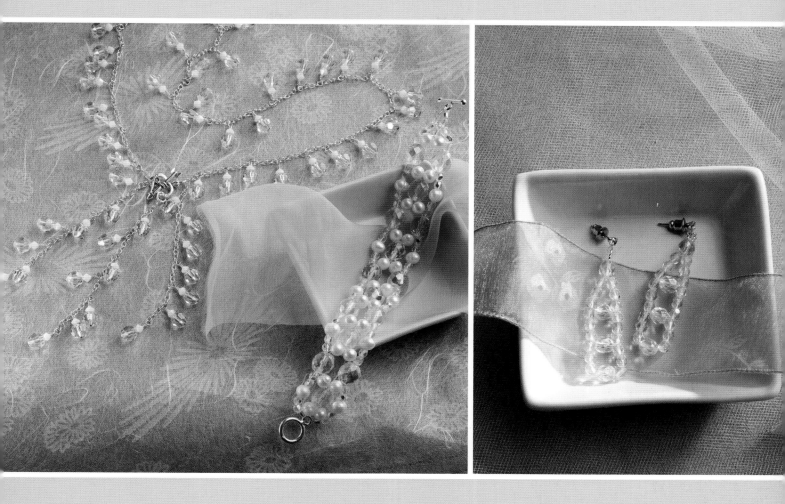

$\mathcal{F}$or most brides, the star of wedding-day jewelry is the ring. But the other accessories you wear can make an impact, too. A piece of jewelry or a pretty bag can enhance your complete bridal look, creating dots of sparkle and complementing your dress and headpiece.

Words from the Wedding Planner

Understand your dress's style before you make any accessories for it. Chances are that grandma's antique lace gown won't look any better with a starkly modern necklace than your Vera Wang will with a frilly, old-fashioned one. Choose necklaces that complement your dress's neckline and frame your face, bracelets that coordinate with the sleeves of your dress, and earrings that work well with your headpiece and hairstyle.

If you're having a hard time discerning your dress's style, ask your best friend to work it out with you, or, better yet, get some advice from a bridal shop employee.

Tying the Knot Pearl Necklace

This is the most classic of pearl necklaces. You can wear it on your wedding day, and you will evoke Grace Kelly every time you wear it afterwards.

Materials and Tools

1 strand of potato-shaped 6mm white freshwater pearl beads
2 silver knot cups
Silver fishhook clasp
Silk cord with twisted wire needle
Scissors
Large sewing needle

Step 1: Attach a knot cup to the end of the cord (see page 7).

Step 2: String 1 bead and tie a knot close to the bead. Repeat until you reach the desired length.

Note: You may find it difficult to get the knot close to the beads. There's a trick! Begin by forming a loose overhand knot (Figure 1). Put the needle through the knot and snug it against the bead (Figure 2). Begin pulling on the thread to tighten the knot, keeping the needle that holds the thread stable against the bead (Figure 3). Tighten the knot and remove the needle (Figure 4).

Step 3: Add a knot cup. Connect each of the knot cups to the clasp.

Step 4: Use the other wire end to string 1 crimp tube and the jump ring. Pass back through the tube, but don't crimp it yet.

Step 5: Test to see if the necklace fits as you'd like it to. Adjust the fit as necessary and crimp the tube. Trim any excess wire close to the tube.

Quick & Easy Ideas

❀ Make a delicate necklace by stringing one sparkly crystal on a tiny chain and add a small clasp.

❀ If you have pierced ears, update grandma's old clip earrings by removing the clip and adding an ear wire or post.

❀ String an existing necklace through a white trifold wallet and you've got an instant beaded wedding purse.

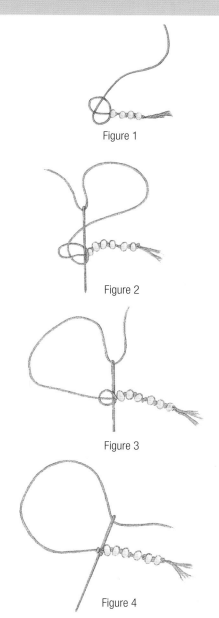

Figure 1

Figure 2

Figure 3

Figure 4

Tumbling Peridot and Pearl Necklace

This version of the classic pearl necklace adds a pretty splash of color to your neckline.

Materials and Tools

1 strand of 6mm white freshwater pearls

20 small peridot stone chips

2 round 3mm sterling silver beads

5mm sterling silver soldered ring

7 sterling silver 1" head pins (thin enough to pass through pearls)

7 sterling silver 1" eye pins (thin enough to pass through peridot)

8mm toggle clasp

2 crimp tubes

Beading wire

Round-nose pliers

Needle-nose pliers

Wire cutters

Crimping pliers

Step 1: String 1 chip on 1 eye pin. Make a wrapped loop (see page 12) that captures the soldered ring. Repeat four times so you end up with 5 peridot dangles on the soldered ring.

Step 2: String 3 chips on 1 eye pin and make a simple loop (see page 12) to secure the beads. Connect the eye pin to the third dangle hanging from the soldered ring.

Step 3: String 3 chips on 1 eye pin and make a simple loop to secure the beads. Connect this dangle to the bottom of the one you just added.

Step 4: String 1 pearl and 2 chips on a head pin and make a wrapped loop to secure them. Repeat three times so you have 4 dangles in all. Connect 1 dangle to the second dangle you made in Step 1 and 1 dangle to the fourth dangle you made

in Step 1. Connect 1 dangle to the bottom of the dangle placed in Step 2 and 1 dangle on the other side of this same loop.

Step 5: String 1 pearl on 1 head pin and make a wrapped loop. Repeat two times so you have 3 dangles in all. Connect 1 dangle to the bottom of the dangle you added in Step 3. Connect the other 2 dangles to the 2 outside peridot chip dangles you made in Step 1.

Step 6: Cut a 20" length of wire. String the soldered ring on the wire and slide it to the center.

Step 7: String pearls on both sides of the wire until you reach your desired length. Finish the strands with 1 silver round and 1 crimp tube on each end.

Step 8: Crimp the wire ends to each side of the clasp (see page 11).

Pearlized Chain Necklace

Suzy Cox

This simple necklace is very modern and quite pretty when worn. It could also work well for a bridesmaid if you use different-colored pearls or exchange the pearls for other types of beads.

Materials and Tools

10" of 3×5mm sterling silver chain

6 potato-shaped 6mm freshwater pearl beads

20" of silver beading wire

5×8mm sterling silver lobster clasp

6mm sterling silver jump ring

2 sterling silver crimp tubes

Wire cutters

Crimping pliers

Note: Be sure that your beading wire will fit through the holes of your pearls. If not, buy a thinner wire.

Step 1: Cut the chain into five 2" pieces and fold each in half. Set aside.

Step 2: Use the wire to string 1 pearl and 1 piece of chain at the fold. Repeat until you add all the pearls and chain. End with a pearl.

Step 3: String 1 crimp tube and the lobster clasp. Pass back through the tube so you have a 1" tail. Snug the tube and crimp it (see page 11).

Flapper Bride Pearls

Strung with thread, then knotted and glued, this pearl necklace won't go scattering across the floor if it breaks. Wear it as a long-flowing drape, wrap it several times around your neck, or tie it to make a *sautoir*.

Materials and Tools

5 strands of white potato-shaped freshwater pearls

1 size 8° seed bead

White Power Pro 10# test

G-S Hypo Cement

Size 12 beading needle

Children's Fiskars scissors

Step 1: Use a 6' length of thread to string the seed bead, leaving a 5" tail. Pass through it again. This is your tension bead.

Step 2: Tie several overhand knots in the thread about 1" apart from each other (Figure 1).

Step 3: String the pearls, pushing them over the overhand knots (Figure 2). Tie more knots in the unstrung portion of the thread as you continue.

Step 4: Use several square knots to tie the beginning and end of the thread together. Pass the working and tail threads back through the pearls to hide the thread.

Step 5: Glue the knots and let dry. Add a drop of glue on the thread every 10 or so pearls so they stick to the line (Figure 3).

Figure 1

Figure 2

Figure 3

Gentlewoman Collar

Arlene Baker

This elegant woven necklace is reminiscent of the pearl chokers or "dog collars" that became the height of fashion during the early part of the twentieth century.

Materials and Tools

180 round 5mm glass pearl beads
10 round 6mm glass pearl beads
58 round 7mm glass pearl beads
1 round 8mm glass pearl bead
1 brass 1" head pin
10 brass 1" eye pins
2 brass 1" three-loop connectors
1 brass fishhook clasp
2" piece of silver French wire (gimp)
1 spool of white nylon beading thread
8" x 11" piece of foam core board
Transparent tape
Scissors
Tape measure or ruler
Straight pins
12 twisted wire needles
Wire cutters
Round-nose pliers
Needle-nose pliers

For a 12" necklace.

Step 1: Tape the piece of foam core board to your work surface. Pin 1 connector to side of the foam core so the 3 loops point toward the center of the board.

Step 2: Cut six 72" lengths of thread and six ³⁄₁₆" pieces of French wire.

Step 3: Thread one of the needles with two lengths of thread, leaving a 2" tail. String one piece of French wire and slide it to the middle of the threads. Pass through the first of the connector's loops so the French wire wraps around the loop. Adjust the thread until the four ends are even (Figure 1).

Figure 1

Step 4: Rethread the twisted wire needle using all four ends as one. String two 5mm pearls.

Step 5: Repeat Steps 3 and 4 using the four remaining lengths of thread.

Step 6: Use one thread from the left loop to string one 7mm pearl. Use one thread from the middle loop to pass back through the pearl you just strung. Pull tight.

Step 7: Use one thread from the right loop to string one 7mm pearl. Use one (new) thread from the middle loop to pass back through the pearl you just strung. Pull tight.

Step 8: Use the four threads that extend from the left loop to string two 5mm pearls. Slide the pearls next to the first 7mm strung and pull tight. Repeat for the center and right loop threads (Figure 2).

Figure 2

Step 9: Repeat Steps 6–8 until you've strung all of the 7mm pearls. Be sure to tighten the weaving each time you add a pearl.

Step 10: Finish the weaving by first stringing two 5mm pearls on the left loop's four threads. String one piece of French wire on all four threads and pass through the corresponding loop on the second connector. Pass back through the last two 5mm pearls strung and pull tight. Use the threads to tie knots between the pearls all along the left side of the necklace. Be sure that each of the four threads is secured by at least two knots. Try to keep the knots hidden within the pearls. Repeat this step for the middle and right loop threads.

Step 11: String the 8mm pearl on a head pin and make a simple loop close to the pearl. Set the dangle aside.

Step 12: String one 6mm pearl on an eye pin and secure it with a simple loop. Set aside. Repeat until you've made ten 6mm pearl links.

Step 13: Connect the 8mm pearl dangle and one of the pearl links. Connect the last link with another one. Continue connecting links until you have a chain made up of one 8mm and six 6mm pearls. Connect the chain to one end of the necklace.

Step 14: Use the rest of the 6mm pearl links to make chain as before. Add the hook clasp to one end, and connect the other end to the necklace.

Lacy Lovely Collarette

Arlene Baker

This netted pearl necklace or "collarette" recalls necklaces created in the 1940s, when glamorous style and fashionable elegance were a part of everyday life.

Materials and Tools

67 round 6mm pearl beads (large)

67 round 4mm pearl beads (medium)

497 round 3mm pearl beads (small)

4 silver 2mm jump or split rings

4 silver 2mm soldered or split rings

Rhinestone-studded two-holed fishhook clasp

Size B white nylon beading thread

Scissors

Beading needle

Measuring tape or ruler

Small piece of cardboard

Needle-nose pliers

Wire cutters

For a 16" necklace.

Step 1: Cut a 62" length of thread, fold it in half, and attach it to 1 soldered ring using a lark's head knot (see page 17).

Step 2: Thread both ends of the thread onto the needle, leaving a 4" tail. String 67 large pearls. *Note*: To ensure a proper fit, wrap the strand of beads around your neck where you'd like it to fit. Add 1" to compensate for the clasp. Next, add or subtract two 6mm pearls at a time until the necklace fits properly.

Remove the needle and wrap the extra thread around the cardboard so you can keep the thread out of the way as you work the netting.

Step 3: Cut a 62" length of thread. Fold it in half and attach it to 1 soldered ring using a lark's head knot. Thread both ends of the thread onto the needle, leaving a 4" tail. String 8 small pearls, 1 medium pearl, 2 small pearls, 1 medium pearl, 2 small pearls, 1 medium pearl, and 2 small pearls. These are pearls 1 through 17.

Step 4: Pass back through pearls 6 through 4 to make a loop. String 2 small pearls. Pass through the third bead of the large-bead strand (Figure 1). This is your first net.

Step 5: String 8 small pearls and pass back through pearl 15 from the last net. String 2 small pearls, 1 medium pearl, 2 small pearls, 1 medium pearl, and 2 small pearls. Pass back up through pearls 5 through 3 added in this step. String 2 small pearls. Skip a bead on the large-bead strand and pass through the next (Figure 1).

Step 6: Repeat Step 5 to make a series of nets off of the large-bead strand. When you make the last net, end the sequence with 3 small pearls instead of 2. End the thread by stringing 1 soldered ring and pushing it down against the last pearl. Loop around the ring again, pass back through the last pearl, and pull tight. Tie two tight overhand knots around the thread between the last 2 pearls and pass back through a couple more pearls. Tie another two tight knots. Continue in this manner, weaving back through the nets and knotting between pearls until the beads are securely fastened. Trim the thread close to the beads.

Step 7: Carefully unwrap the large-bead strand's working thread and use both thread ends to thread a needle. Make sure that 2 large pearls end the strand. End the thread by stringing a jump ring and pushing it down against the last pearl. Loop around the ring again, pass back through the last 3 pearls on the strand, and pull tight. Tie knots between pearls as you did before until the thread is securely fastened. Trim the thread close to the beads.

Step 8: Attach 1 jump ring to each soldered ring at the ends of the necklace. Attach the jump rings to the clasp loops.

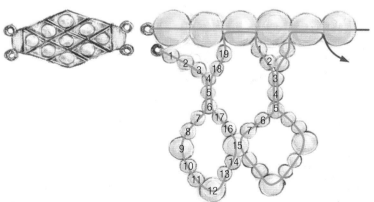

Figure 1

Chained Melody Necklace

Suzy Cox

The color of the beads on this bridesmaid's necklace can be changed to suit your wedding palette, and changing the glass pearls to semiprecious stones or crystals would give it a completely different look.

Materials and Tools

18" of 3×5mm sterling silver chain
6 round 8mm Swarovski glass pearl beads
5 round 6mm Swarovski glass pearl beads
11 sterling silver 2" head pins
6×11mm sterling silver lobster clasp
Round-nose pliers
Needle-nose pliers
Wire cutters

Step 1: Fold the chain so there is 8" on one half and 10" on the other. Take note of the link that falls where you made the fold. Set on your work surface.

Step 2: String 1 small pearl on a head pin. Make a wrapped loop (see page 12) that captures the link you marked in Step 1.

Step 3: Count 5 chain links to one side of the dangle you just placed and place another one, this time using 1 large pearl.

Step 4: Continue up one side of the chain until you've added 3 large and 2 small pearls. Repeat up the other side of the chain.

Step 5: Attach the lobster clasp to one end of the chain. Attach the clasp to any point on the chain so that the wearer can adjust the size. If desired, add one more small pearl to the very end of the chain.

Jumbled Jewels

This delicate ribbon choker is punctuated with a jumble of crystals that nestle comfortably in the dip in your neck, or, as the French call it, *le décolletage*.

Materials and Tools

28 round 8mm crystal AB Austrian crystal beads

2 round 3mm sterling silver beads

2 saucer-shaped 5mm sterling silver beads

7 sterling silver 7mm soldered rings

26 sterling silver 2" head pins

1 sterling silver 1" eye pin

12mm sterling silver toggle clasp

15" of ⅝" organza ribbon

Fray Check

Needle-nose pliers

Round-nose pliers

Wire cutters

Step 1: Use a head pin to string 1 crystal bead. Make a wrapped loop (see page 12) that captures 1 soldered ring. Repeat twice, so you have 3 dangles on the ring.

Step 2: Repeat Step 1 four times so you end up with 5 soldered rings with 3 dangles each.

Step 3: Repeat Step 1 twice, this time adding 5 dangles to each ring.

Step 4: Use the eye pin to string 1 crystal bead. Make a wrapped loop that captures one of the 3-dangle soldered rings.

Step 5: Use a head pin to string 1 round silver bead, 1 saucer silver bead, 1 crystal bead, 1 saucer silver bead, 1 round silver bead, and 1 crystal. Make a wrapped loop that captures the eye of the eye pin placed in the previous step.

Step 6: Pass the end of the ribbon through the loop on the ring end of the clasp and tie a strong knot, leaving a 1½" tail. String the soldered rings onto the ribbon in this sequence: two 3-dangle soldered rings, one 5-dangle soldered rings, the soldered ring with the long dangle, one 5-dangle soldered ring, and two 3-dangle soldered rings. Slide the rings to the middle of the ribbon.

Step 7: Wrap the ribbon around your neck where you'd like it to fit, mark the place where the bar end of the clasp should go, remove the ribbon from your neck, and use a strong knot to tie the bar to the ribbon.

Step 8: Trim one ribbon end at an angle about 1" from the knot that ties it to the clasp. Dab the end of the ribbon with Fray Check. Repeat for the other ribbon end.

Classic Illusion Necklace

Suzy Cox

This classic necklace style is perfect for adding extra glimmer and won't detract from a dress. The one shown here is for a bridesmaid, but make it with clear crystals, and you've got the perfect bride's necklace.

Materials and Tools

9 round 8mm Swarovski crystal beads
18 bicone 4mm Swarovski crystal beads
20 sterling silver crimp tubes
20" of medium silver beading wire
5×8mm sterling silver lobster clasp
6mm sterling silver jump ring
2" of 3×5mm sterling silver chain
Wire cutters
Crimping pliers

For an 18" necklace.

Step 1: String 1 crimp tube, 1 bicone, 1 round, 1 bicone, and 1 crimp tube. Slide all the beads to the center of the wire so the round sits dead center. Snug the beads together and crimp the tubes (see page 11) to keep everything in place.

Step 2: Use one wire end to string 1 crimp tube. Slide it so that it is about 1" from the last crimp tube. Crimp the tube. String 1 bicone, 1 round, 1 bicone, and 1 tube. Snug the beads and crimp the tube. Repeat this step for the other side of the necklace.

Step 3: Repeat Step 2 until you've added all the beads and crimp tubes, added evenly to both sides of the first central set.

Step 4: String 1 crimp tube and the lobster clasp. Pass back through the tube so you have a 1" tail. Snug the tube but don't crimp it yet.

Step 5: Use the other wire end to string 1 crimp tube and the jump ring. Pass back through the tube but don't crimp it yet.

Step 6: Test to see if the necklace fits as you'd like it to. Adjust the fit as necessary and crimp the tubes. Trim any excess wire close to the tubes.

Double-Take Necklace

Suzy Cox

This double-stranded necklace gives the illusion that there are beads floating around your neck. It's been a favorite for brides I've met and is also lovely as a bridesmaid's necklace.

Materials and Tools
for an 18" necklace

15 round 6mm Swarovski crystal beads
15 potato-shaped 6mm freshwater pearl beads
16 sterling silver crimp tubes
40" of fine silver beading wire
5×8mm sterling silver lobster clasp
6mm sterling silver jump ring
Wire cutters
Crimping pliers

Note: Be sure that your beading wire will fit through the holes of your pearls. If not, buy a thinner wire.

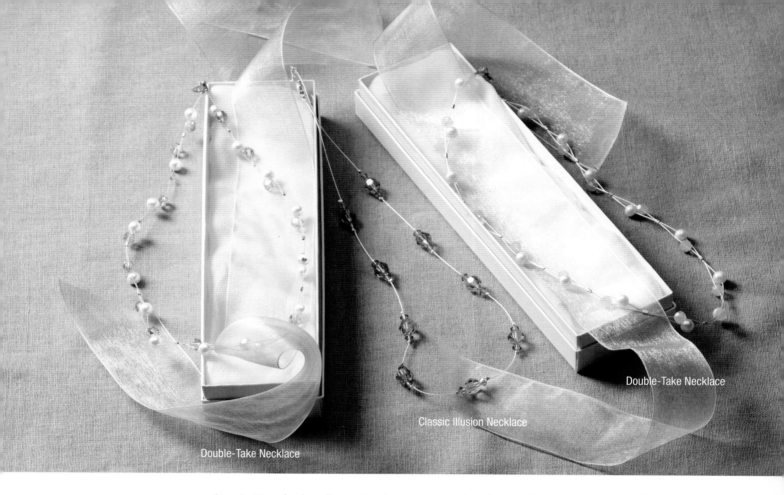

Double-Take Necklace

Classic Illusion Necklace

Double-Take Necklace

Figure 1

Step 1: Cut the beading wire into two equal lengths.

Step 2: String 1 pearl on one wire and slide it to the middle. String 1 crystal on the other wire and slide it to the middle. Pair one end of each wire with the other and string 1 crimp tube. Pair the other ends of the wires and string 1 crimp tube. The crimps should be on either side of the beads (Figure 1), and the whole configuration should sit in the center of the wires, with the crimp tubes about 1¼" apart. Crimp the tubes (see page 11).

Step 3: Working from one end, string 1 pearl on one wire and 1 crystal on the other wire. Pair the wire ends and string 1 crimp tube. Slide the tube so that it's about 1¼" from the last crimp tube, and crimp it. Repeat for the other side of the necklace.

Step 4: Repeat Step 3, adding beads and crimping the tube on one side of the necklace, and doing the same on the other, until you've added 13 bead sets in all.

Step 5: For the last set of beads, string 1 pearl and 1 crystal on each wire. Pair the ends and string 1 crimp tube. Pass the wire ends through the loop on the lobster clasp and back through the tube but don't crimp yet. Repeat for the other side of the necklace using the jump ring. Test to see if the necklace fits as you'd like it to. Adjust the fit as necessary and crimp the tubes. Trim any excess wire close to the tubes.

Wisteria Necklace

Suzy Cox

This less traditional "wowza" necklace is for a dress with a plunging neckline.

Materials and Tools

40" of 2×3mm sterling silver chain
58 round 8mm Rosaline Swarovski crystal beads
58 bicone 4mm alabaster Swarovski crystal beads
58 sterling silver 2" head pins
Sterling silver heart toggle clasp
Round-nose pliers
Needle-nose pliers
Wire cutters

Step 1: Cut 4" of chain and set aside.

Step 2: Make a bead dangle by stringing 1 round and 1 bicone on a head pin. Make a wrapped loop (see page 12) that captures the end link on the long piece of chain. Count 7 links up the chain and add another dangle. Continue all along the chain until you've added 52 dangles.

Step 3: Make a bead dangle on the end of the short chain, count 7 links up the chain, and add another dangle. Continue all along the chain until you've added 6 dangles.

Step 4: Put a jump ring on the ring side of the clasp and attach it to the long chain between the eighth and ninth dangles added. Put a jump ring on the bar side of the clasp and attach it to the chain between the forty-fourth and forty-third dangles added.

Step 5: Put a jump ring on the open-end link of the short chain and attach it to the ring side of the clasp (Figure 1).

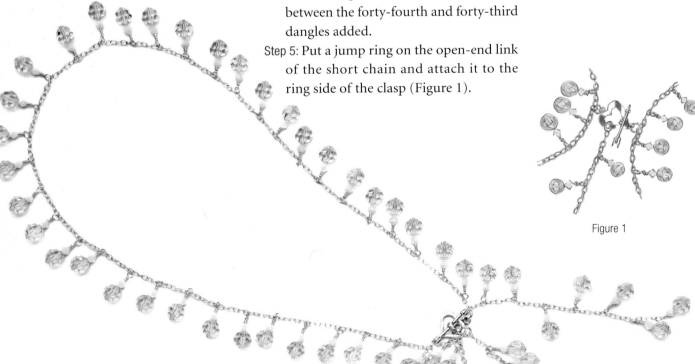

Figure 1

Princess Cuffington Bracelet, page 106

Pearlie Girl Ensemble

This pearl ensemble would look great with a simple wedding dress, but the necklace and earrings also make a really nice mother-of-the-bride ensemble. Wear it loose or twist or braid it for a tighter look.

Materials and Tools for Necklace

3 strands of potato-shaped 6mm white freshwater pearl beads

16 flat square 8×10mm light pink freshwater pearl beads

6 flat oval 10×12mm light pink freshwater pearl beads

11 round 4mm light rose Czech fire-polished beads

6 sterling silver crimp tubes

Sterling silver double-hook clasp

Beading wire thin enough to pass through the pearls

Wire cutters

Crimping pliers

Bead Stoppers

Step 1: Cut three 20" lengths of beading wire. Use crimp tubes to attach each to one side of the clasp, leaving less than 1" tails. Once crimped (see page 11), trim the tails close to the tube.

Step 2: Use one wire to string 3 potato pearls. Next, string 1 square pearl and 3 potato pearls sixteen times. Use a Bead Stopper to temporarily hold the beads in place.

Step 3: Use the second wire to string 10 potato pearls. Next, string 1 oval pearl and 10 potato pearls eleven times. Stop the beads as before.

Step 4: Use the third wire to string 6 potato pearls. Next, string 1 fire-polished bead and 6 potato pearls eleven times. Stop the beads as before.

Step 5: Hold the beads up to determine if all the strands are equal in length. Adjust the strands as necessary by adding or subtracting beads from the end. Don't worry too much about keeping the stringing patterns exact.

Step 6: Use crimp tubes to attach the strands to the other side of the clasp. Trim the wire tails close to the tubes.

Materials and Tools for Earrings

2 flat oval 10×12mm light pink freshwater pearl beads

2 round 6mm light rose Czech fire-polished beads

2 sterling silver 2" head pins

Pair of sterling silver ear wires

Round-nose pliers

Needle-nose pliers

Wire cutters

Step 1: String 1 oval and 1 fire-polished on a head pin and secure the beads with a wrapped loop (see page 12).

Step 2: Hook the dangle on the ear wire.

Step 3: Repeat all to make a second earring.

Sophisticate Bracelet

This beauty has just enough sparkle to make it exciting but just enough polish to grant an understated elegance.

Materials and Tools

8 round 6mm crystal AB Austrian crystal beads

18 potato-shaped gunmetal AB freshwater pearl beads

18 sterling silver 5mm flat rondelles

2 sterling silver 3mm seamless round beads

11mm sterling silver toggle clasp

2 sterling silver crimp tubes

10" of flexible beading wire

Wire cutters

Crimping pliers

Step 1: String 1 crimp tube and pass the wire end through the loop on the ring side of the clasp. Pass back through the crimp tube, and crimp (see page 11), leaving less than a 1" tail. String 1 sterling silver round.

Step 2: String 1 rondelle, 2 pearls, 1 rondelle, and 1 crystal. Repeat the sequence seven times so you place all 8 crystals. End the strand by stringing 1 rondelle, 2 pearls, 1 rondelle, and 1 sterling silver round.

Step 3: String 1 crimp tube. Pass through the loop on the bar side of the clasp and back through the tube. Snug the beads and crimp. Trim any excess wire close to the beads.

Last-Minute Bracelet

I designed this bracelet in minutes. You can make it in even less time, and it makes a great gift for that last-minute guest who has arrived for the big day!

Materials and Tools

6 round flat 8mm two-holed spacer beads with Swarovski rhinestone inset

56 round 4mm crystal AB Swarovski crystal beads

1 sterling silver 3mm round bead

2 sterling silver crimp tubes

10mm sterling silver toggle clasp

Beading wire

Step 1: Cut one 20" length of wire. String the ring side of the clasp and slide it to the center of the wire. Use both ends to string 1 crimp tube. Snug the tube and crimp it (see page 11).

Step 2: String 4 beads on each wire. String the spacer bead. Repeat five times. String 4 beads on each wire.

Step 3: Pair the wire ends and string through the silver bead and 1 crimp tube. Pass both of the ends through the bar side of the clasp and back through the tube. Snug the beads and crimp. Trim the excess wire close to the tube.

Sophisticate Bracelet

Last-Minute Bracelet

Last-Minute Bracelet

Sophisticate Bracelet

Champagne Bracelet

This bubbly bracelet is a nice one for bridesmaids to wear. Simply change the color scheme to complement their dresses.

Materials and Tools

6 round 10mm Czech fire-polished beads

12 faceted 8mm flat rondelle beads

5 bicone 4mm Austrian crystal beads

12 sterling silver 3mm seamless round beads

11mm sterling silver toggle clasp

2 sterling silver crimp tubes

10" of flexible beading wire

Wire cutters

Crimping pliers

Step 1: String 1 crimp tube and pass the wire end through the loop on the ring side of the clasp. Pass back through the crimp tube and crimp (see page 11), leaving less than a 1" tail.

Step 2: String 1 sterling silver round bead, 1 rondelle, one 10mm, 1 rondelle, 1 sterling silver round, and 1 crystal. Repeat the sequence four times. End the strand by stringing 1 sterling silver round, 1 rondelle, one 10mm, 1 rondelle, and 1 sterling silver round.

Step 3: String 1 crimp tube. Pass through the loop on the bar side of the clasp and back through the tube. Snug the beads and crimp. Trim any excess wire close to the beads.

Champagne Bracelet

Dannikka's Bracelet

Dannikka's Bracelet

My sister-in-law, Dannikka, might like to have worn this bracelet in her wedding to my brother, but I designed it for her a few years too late!

Materials and Tools

12 potato-shaped 5mm freshwater pearl beads
12 Thai silver 6½mm rondelles
2 sterling silver 3mm seamless round beads
25 round 6mm Austrian crystal beads
15 sterling silver head pins
5 sterling silver 7mm soldered or split rings
11mm sterling silver toggle clasp
2 sterling silver crimp tubes
10" of flexible beading wire
Round-nose pliers
Needle-nose pliers
Wire cutters

Step 1: Use a head pin to string 1 crystal. Make a wrapped loop (see page 12) that captures one of the soldered rings. Make two more bead dangles in this manner on the same ring.

Step 2: Repeat Step 1 four times so you end up with 5 rings with 3 dangles each. Set aside.

Step 3: String 1 crimp tube and pass the wire end through the loop on the ring side of the clasp. Pass back through the crimp tube and crimp (see page 11), leaving less than a 1" tail. String 1 sterling silver round.

Step 4: String 1 rondelle, 2 pearls, 1 rondelle, 1 crystal, 1 of the beaded rings, and 1 crystal. Repeat the sequence four times. End the strand by stringing 1 rondelle, 2 pearls, 1 rondelle, and 1 sterling silver round.

Step 5: String 1 crimp tube. Pass through the loop on the bar side of the clasp and back through the tube. Snug the beads and crimp. Trim any excess wire close to the beads.

Princess Cuffington Bracelet

This woven cuff bracelet would look stunning with a sleeveless dress—just the thing to attract attention down your arm and to your ring!

Materials and Tools for an 8" bracelet

49 round 4mm crystal AB Czech fire-polished beads

11 round 10mm crystal AB Czech fire-polished beads

32 round or potato 6mm white freshwater pearl beads

4 sterling silver crimp tubes

Sterling silver 12mm toggle clasp

48" of medium sterling silver beading wire

Wire cutters

Crimping pliers

Step 1: Cut the beading wire into two 24" pieces. Take one wire and pass it through the loop on the ring side of the clasp. Pair the wire ends and string 1 crimp tube. Slide the tube along the wires until you reach the clasp loop. Crimp the tube (see page 11). Repeat for the other wire.

There should be four wires coming from the clasp now, Wires 1 through 4.

Step 2: Use Wire 1 to string two 4mm, 1 pearl, and two 4mm. Use Wire 2 to string 1 pearl, one 10mm, and 1 pearl. Use Wire 3 to string 1 pearl, pass through the 10mm just strung on Wire 2, and string 1 pearl. Use Wire 4 to string two 4mm, 1 pearl, and two 4mm.

Pair Wires 1 and 2 and string one 10mm. Pair Wires 3 and 4 and string one 10mm. Snug the beads to the clasp and pull all the wires very tight so the beads arrange themselves in the design shown on Figure 1.

Figure 1

Step 3: Repeat Step 2 four times.

Step 4: Use Wire 1 to string three 4mm. Use Wire 2 to string 1 pearl and one 4mm. Use Wire 3 to string 1 pearl and pass through the 4mm just strung on Wire 2. Use Wire 4 to string three 4mm.

Step 5: Pair Wires 1 and 2 and string one 4mm and 1 crimp tube. Pair Wires 3 and 4 and string one 4mm and 1 crimp tube. Snug all the beads on the entire bracelet so they are arranged neatly in place.

Figure 2

Pass the Wire 1 and 2 ends through the loop on the bar end of the clasp and back through the crimp tube. Repeat for Wires 3 and 4 (Figure 2). Snug the crimp tubes.

Step 6: Test to make sure the bracelet fits. If not, remove the beads added in Steps 4 and 5. Add or subtract beads as necessary in Step 3 and then work through the rest of the instructions. Be sure to test the bracelet size again.

Step 7: Snug the beads, crimp the tubes, and trim the wire close to the beads.

Words from the Wedding Planner

Whether you have long or short hair, pierced ears or not, earrings are a must-have for any wedding ensemble. They draw attention to your face and can definitely be a complement to your headpiece. Crystals and pearls are the classic materials for wedding jewelry, especially for a bride's earrings. Here are several ideas for pairing the two materials. Let them inspire you to make your own designs!

Note: While you're at the bead shop, check to see that the head pins you buy go through the pearls you're using. A 22- to 24-gauge head pin usually works best.

Cascade Earrings

This style of earrings has been a favorite of the brides I've met who have a more understated headpiece or are just wearing a comb or bobby pins.

Materials and Tools

14 round 6mm crystal AB Swarovski crystal beads
14 sterling silver 1" head pins
Pair of French ear wires or earring posts and nuts

Step 1: String 1 bead on 1 head pin. Make a simple loop (see page 12) at the end of the head pin (the bead will move freely, but shouldn't fall off of the head pin). Set aside.

Step 2: String 1 bead on 1 head pin. Pass the head pin through the loop on the head pin from Step 1 (Figure 1). Make a simple loop on the end of this head pin (Figure 2). Repeat twice so you end up with a chain of 4 beaded head pins. Set aside.

Step 3: Repeat Steps 1 and 2 to make a chain of 3 beaded head pins.

Step 4: Open the loop on the earring finding and hook on the 2 head pin chains. Close the loop.

Step 5: Repeat all to make a second earring.

Figure 1

Figure 2

Stairway to Heaven Earrings

These woven chandelier earrings are dramatic but don't take a drastic amount of time.

Materials and Tools

8 round 6mm Czech fire-polished beads (large)
36 round 4mm Czech fire-polished beads (small)
12 size 14° seed beads
2 ear posts and ear nuts
Power Pro line
Size 12 beading needle
Children's Fiskars scissors
Match or melting tool
Nail polish

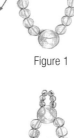

Figure 1

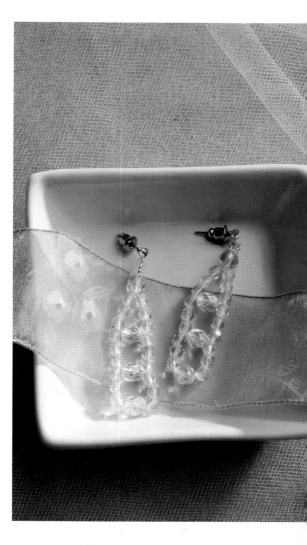

Step 1: Use an 18" length of thread to string 6 seed beads, 1 large round bead, 9 small round beads, 1 large round bead, and 9 small round beads.

Step 2: Pass back through the first large round bead added in Step 1. Pass through the seed beads, the first large round, and the first 3 small rounds added in Step 1 (Figure 1).

Step 3: String a large round and pass through the last 3 small rounds added in Step 1. Pass back through the first large round added in Step 1 and through the 6 seed beads, first large round, and 6 small rounds added in Step 1 (Figure 2).

Step 4: String a large round and pass through the last 6 small rounds added in Step 1. Pass back through the large round added in the previous step and through the seventh to ninth small beads added in Step 1 (Figure 3).

Figure 2

Figure 3

Step 5: Pass through all the beads again to reinforce. Tie the tail and working threads together. Burn the knot and use nail polish to seal it.

Step 6: Open the loop on the earring finding and hook on the earring. Close the loop.

Step 7: Repeat all to make a second earring.

Bride Carolyn's Wedding Purse

Sandi Wiseheart

Little did Bride Carolyn know that her request to Sister Sandi to make a bag to match her wedding dress would result in a beautiful family heirloom.

Only advanced loomworkers should tackle this project. (Don't say I didn't warn you!)

Materials and Tools

Delica beads:

  100 g of opaque white AB (A)

  3 g of clear crystal (B)

  5 g white opal

  5 g matte metallic silver

50 oval 3mm white freshwater pearls

50 oval 4mm white freshwater pearls

50 oval 4×6mm white freshwater pearls

50 oval 5×7mm white freshwater pearls

100 bicone 3mm clear Swarovski crystals

200 bicone 4mm clear Swarovski crystals

500 round 2mm silver beads for fringe

150 sterling silver or pewter 6mm floral bead caps

4 round 5mm silver-plated split rings for strap

Silver purse frame with 5⅛"-wide inset opening

2 sterling silver or pewter 6mm links for strap

3' silver chain for strap

⅓ yd white silk fabric for lining

Sewing thread

1 spool of Nymo beading thread

Power Pro braided line

Beading needles

Sewing needles

Scissors

Bead loom 5½" wide × 7" long or larger

Pencil

Finished size: 10" × 6½"

Step 1: Follow the loom manufacturer's instructions and use Nymo thread to warp the loom with 95 warp threads.

Step 2: Use A and B beads to follow the chart on page 112 from the top down, making decreases as indicated. Change the initials if necessary for Rows 67–76.

Step 3: Trim the weft thread, leaving a long tail. Carefully cut all the warp threads leaving at least an 8" tail on each. Set the front of the purse aside, laying it flat to avoid distorting the weaving.

Step 4: Repeat Steps 1–3 to make the back of the purse. Rows 104–119 are the bottom of the purse. Work the bottom in the background color, adding your initials and the year if you wish.

Step 5: Lay the two panels on a table with their bottom edges lined up. Join the panels by weaving the bottom threads from the front panel into the beads at the lower edge of the bottom panel, and the threads from the bottom panel into the beads at the lower edge of the front panel. Weave the remaining warp threads into the beadwork.

Lining

Step 6: Lay the stitched-together panels on a piece of clean paper. Use a pencil to trace around the panels ½" away from the edges. Cut the pattern from the paper, pin it to the silk, and cut the silk. Cut two strips of silk 1¾" wide by 7" long to make the sides of the lining.

Step 7: With right sides together, handstitch each side strip along the front, bottom, and back edges with a ½" seam allowance (Figure 1). Miter the corners and ease fullness as needed. Fold all seam allowances toward the main panels (away from sides) and handstitch again ¼" from seam to secure. Trim allowances close to the stitching and set aside.

Figure 1

Top Front

Purse Bottom
chart Rows 104–119

Top Back

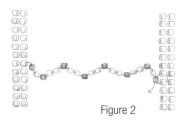

Figure 2

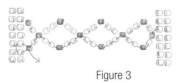

Figure 3

Figure 4

Side-of-Purse Netting

Step 8: Secure a 6' thread in the front panel of the beadwork so it exits 1¼" from the top edge. String 1B, 1A, 1B, 2A, 1B, 2A, 1B, 2A, 1B, 2A, 1B, 2A, 1B, 1A, and 1B, for a total of 20 beads. Pass through the edge bead of the back panel, 2 beads down from the corresponding bead of the front panel. Pass through the edge bead above and through the last B strung (Figure 2). String 1A, 1B, and 2A. Pass back through the sixth B of the previous row. String 2A, 1B, and 2A. Pass back through the fourth B of the previous row. String 2A, 1B, and 2A. Pass back through the second B of the previous row. String 1A and 1B. Pass through the edge bead of the front panel, 4 beads down from the first row, through the edge bead above it, and through the last B strung (Figure 3).

Step 9: String 1A, 1B, and 2A. Pass back through the third B of the previous row. String 2A, 1B, and 2A. Pass back through the second B of the previous row. String 2A, 1B, and 2A. Pass back through the first B of the previous row. String 1A and 1B. Pass through the edge bead of the back panel, 3 beads down from the last edge bead worked, through the edge bead above it, and through the last B strung (Figure 4). Repeat this step, alternating front and back panels, down the side of the bag; end at the bottom panel.

Step 10: Repeat Steps 8 and 9 for the other side of the bag.

Fringe

Step 11: Secure 6' of braided line in the front panel to exit the edge at the top of one slanted side. String 1 silver round, one 4mm crystal, 1 silver round, 23 white opal Delicas, 1 silver round, one 4mm pearl, 1 silver round, one 4mm crystal, 1 bead cap, one 5×7mm pearl, 1 bead cap, one 4mm crystal, and 1 silver round. Skipping the last silver round, pass back through all the beads and into the edge bead of the next row. Pass through 2 beads and exit the next row's edge bead. Repeat this step for 14 fringes along each slanted edge and 22 along the bottom edge.

Step 12: Repeat Step 11 for the back of the bag, stringing 1 silver round, one 4mm crystal, 1 silver round, 30 white opal Delicas, 1 silver round, one 3mm crystal, one 3mm pearl, one 3mm crystal, 1 bead cap, one 4×6mm pearl, and 1 silver round for each fringe.

Finishing

Step 13: Turn the lining wrong side out. Use long pins to pin the lining into the purse with wrong sides facing, folding the top seam allowance under and easing to fit as needed. Sew the lining to the panels between the first and second rows of beads along the top and side edges, and along the first row of netting.

Step 14: Sew the loomwork firmly to the purse frame, passing through beads rather than looping around the warp threads. The netting will reach about ½" up inside the frame. Repeat the stitching at least twice to make sure the beadwork is securely attached.

Step 15: Attach each pewter bead to two split rings. Attach the rings to the chain and purse frame.

SOSNSBSB Bag

You can sew a lining into this tiny miser's bag so you can hold things in it. Or, even better, simply make the netted portion and put your Aunt Nora's blue antique hanky inside it. Then you'll have SOSNSBSB (something old, something new, something borrowed, something blue) covered, and right at your fingertips!

Materials and Tools

Size 11 crystal silver-lined seed beads
112 bicone 4mm black diamond AB Swarovski crystal beads
½" light blue organza ribbon
White Nymo D beading thread
Beading or sharps needle
Scissors

Note: See Figure 1 for bead counts and placement for Steps 1–7.

Step 1: Using a 3' length of thread and leaving a 4" tail, string 3 seed beads and 1 crystal thirty-two times. Pass through the beads again to make a circle and tie a knot. This is your base round. Exit from a crystal.

Step 2: String 6 seed beads, 1 crystal, 20 seed beads, 1 crystal, and 20 seed beads. Pass back through the first crystal strung in this step. String 6 seed beads, skip a crystal on the base round, and pass through the next one.

Step 3: Repeat Step 2 so you end up with 16 nets coming from the base round, each net with a loop attached. Weave through the beads so you exit from a crystal at the bottom of one of the loops.

Step 4: String 6 seed beads, 1 crystal, and 6 seed beads. Pass through the bottom crystal of the next loop added in the previous step. Repeat around until all the loops are connected. Exit from one of the crystals added in this step.

Step 5: String 6 seed beads, 1 crystal, and 6 seed beads. Pass through the bottom crystal of the next net added in the previous step. Repeat around and exit from one of the crystals added in this step.

Step 6: String 9 seed beads, 1 crystal, and 9 seed beads. Pass through the bottom crystal of the next net added in the previous step. Repeat around and exit from one of the crystals added in this step.

Step 7: String 19 seed beads and pass through the bottom crystal of the next net added in the previous step. Repeat around and exit from the tenth bead added in this step.

Note: See Figure 2 for bead counts and placement for Steps 8–12.

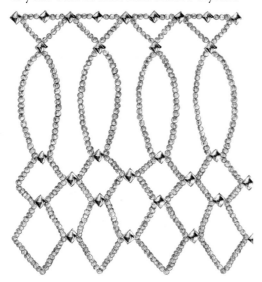

Figure 1

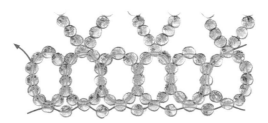

Figure 2

Step 8: String 11 seed beads and pass through the bead you just exited again to form a loop. Continue weaving through the first 4 beads added in this step.

Step 9: String 9 seed beads. Pass through the second, third, and fourth beads from the first loop to make another loop. Pass through the first through sixth beads just added.

Step 10: String 1 seed bead and pass through the tenth bead of the next net added in Step 7. String 7 seed beads and pass through the fourth through sixth beads added in the previous loop. Continue weaving through the first seed bead added in this step, the net bead, and the fourth through sixth bead added in this step.

Step 11: Continue working this single-needle right-angle weave around the bag, attaching the nets with every other loop. Exit from the second bead at the bottom of one of the loops.

Step 12: Tighten the bottom of the bag by stringing 1 seed bead and passing through the second bead at the bottom of the next loop. The loops will ruffle, and you should end up with a ¾" opening at the bottom of the bag.

Step 13: Weave through all of the beads on the bag again to reinforce. Secure the thread and trim close to the work.

Paulette's Brooch

This brooch was inspired by a request from *Beaded Weddings's* ever-savvy art director.

Materials and Tools

1½×2" oval brass screen finding with clip-on beading dome and pin back (available at Ornamental Resources)

1 round 10mm crystal AB Czech fire-polished bead

8 round 6mm crystal AB Czech fire-polished beads

40 round 4mm peridot Czech fire-polished beads

8 potato-shaped 6mm white freshwater pearl beads

16 flat round 15mm pearl buttons with holes on one side

Size 11° rose seed beads

G-S Hypo Cement

26-gauge brass wire

Needle-nose pliers

Wire cutters

Step 1: Attach a wire near the center of the dome so the long part of the wire exits from the top.

Step 2: String the 10mm bead and pass back down into the dome so the bead is placed squarely in the center of the oval.

Step 3: Pass up through the dome right next to the 10mm bead. String 1 pearl. Pass down through the dome and back up again next to the pearl. Continue around, adding all the pearls so they circle the 10mm.

Step 4: Weaving the wire in and out of the dome again, place a round of the 6mm beads. These beads will be adjacent to each pearl. Exit between the 6mms.

Step 5: String 5 seed beads and pass down through the dome again to make a small loop of beads between the 6mms. Exit from a hole right behind one of the loops.

Step 6: String five 4mm beads and pass down through the dome next to where you last exited. Continue around, adding a 4mm-bead loop behind every seed-bead loop.

Step 7: Make a round of 7 seed-bead loops behind each 6mm bead.

Step 8: Make a round of buttons on the very perimeter of the brooch. One half of each button should overlap the next one so that you end up with a tight round. If one of the buttons is floppy, glue it to the next button.

Madamoiselle's Brooch

Arlene Baker

Vintage-inspired, with lustrous faux pearls and sparkling glass beads, this dazzlingly feminine pin can be worn anywhere—even on your shoes!

Materials and Tools

42 round 6mm light sapphire Czech fire-polished beads

28 round 4mm light sapphire Czech fire-polished beads

21 round 3mm light sapphire Czech fire-polished beads

224 round 2.5mm white glass pearl beads

28 round 3mm white glass pearl beads

1 round 12mm white glass pearl bead

1 spool of 28-gauge silver craft wire

1 spool of 26-gauge silver craft wire

2 round 1⅜" filigrees (matching), one flat and one curved

1" pin clasp with two holes

Wire cutters

Wire straighteners

Needle-nose pliers

Round-nose pliers

Tape measure or ruler

Bead mat or bead dish

Wire spool holders

Figure 1

Step 1: Cut forty-two 1½" lengths of the 26-gauge wire and set aside.

Step 2: Take one wire length and turn a simple loop (see page 12) on one end. Use the wire to string one 6mm and one 3mm fire-polished beads. Turn a simple loop to secure the beads. Repeat twenty times so you have 21 small beaded links in all.

Step 3: Repeat Step 2, this time stringing one 6mm and one 4mm fire-polished bead. You should end up with 21 medium beaded links in all.

Step 4: Cut a 13" length of 26-gauge wire. String one 3mm pearl and 1 small link (on the 3mm end). String one 3mm pearl and 1 medium link (on the 4mm end). Repeat this step until you've strung 28 pearls, 14 small links, and 14 medium links.

Step 5: Slide the links and pearls to the middle of the wire (make sure both ends of the wire are even) and cross the wires to make a tight circle. Twist the two wires tightly together for ½"(see page 13). Trim the twisted wires to about ¼". Shape the center of the circle if necessary and bend the trimmed twisted wires toward the center. Beginning near the twisted wires, pull up every small link, leaving the medium links down and flat against your work surface. The resulting circle should look like a ruffle.

Step 6: Cut 34" length of 26-gauge wire and pass it through the exposed loop on the medium link that sits next to the twisted wire. Pull it through the loop until you have a 5" tail. String five 2.5mm pearls and pass through the end loop of the next small link. Pull tight. String five 2.5mm pearls and pass through the end loop of the next medium link. Pull tight. Repeat around the circle so you have a zigzag pattern of pearls around the inner circle. Use your fingers to pinch the wire points to make them sharper and more distinct (Figure 1). End the wire with a ½" twist, trim it to ¼", and bend it toward the center of the circle. This is the outer ruffle. Set aside.

Step 7: Cut a 12" length of 26-gauge wire. String one 2.5mm pearl and 1 small link (on the 3mm end). String one 2.5mm pearl and 1 medium link (on the 4mm end). Repeat this step until you've strung 14 pearls, 7 small links, and 7 medium links. Finish this circle the same way you did the outer ruffle in Steps 5 and 6. This is the inner ruffle. Set aside.

Step 8: Study your filigree and mark eight equidistant points around it. Center the outer ruffle on it.

Step 9: Cut eight 8" lengths of 28-gauge wire and fold each in half. Take one piece of folded wire and straddle it over the inner wire of the outer ruffle at one of the points determined in Step 8. Pull the doubled wire tightly to the back of the filigree, making sure it holds the ruffle down, but is hidden between pearls on the ruffle's inner wire circle. Twist the wire ends for ¼", trim to ⅛", and bend it flat against the filigree toward the center. Repeat around to completely secure the outer ruffle.

Step 10: Cut eight 8" lengths of 28-gauge beading wire and fold each in half. Use these wires to secure the inner ruffle to the center of the filigree as you did the outer ruffle. Make sure the seven "valleys" of the inner ruffle nestle between the seven "peaks" of the outer ruffle.

Step 11: Cut one 10" length of 28-gauge wire. String the 12mm pearl, slide it to the middle of the wire and bend the wires down on each side. Pass the wires down through the center of the filigree to seat the pearl in the middle of the pin. Twist the wires at the back of the filigree for ¼", trim to ⅛", and bend the twist flat against the filigree (Figure 2).

Figure 2

Step 12: Cut seven 8" lengths of 28-gauge wire and fold each in half. Use one wire to string one 4mm bead and pass it down through the filigree underneath one of the peaks of the inner ruffle. Twist, trim, and bend the wires as before (Figure 3). Repeat around.

Step 13: Cut two 8" lengths of 28-gauge wire and fold each in half. Pick up the flat filigree and hold it with the right side (raised or embossed side) facing you. Attach the pin clasp to the filigree in the same way you attached the ruffles. The pin should rest near the top of the filigree, not in the center.

Figure 3

Step 14: Cut four 10" lengths of 28-gauge wire and fold each in half. Line up the two filigrees evenly, with wrong sides together. Use one wire to pass through the flat filigree on through the curve filigree. Twist the wires tightly against the curved filigree for ½" and trim to ¼". Use the round-nose pliers to curve the trimmed twisted wires, then press the curve flat against the front filigree. Repeat to attach the flat and curved filigrees at equidistant points around the pin.

*W*eddings don't happen without the help of others, so it's appropriate to give a small gift to those whose help you truly appreciate. These gifts don't need to be elaborate. They should just serve as a thoughtful reminder to the receiver that you and your spouse are grateful for everything they've done for you. That could include your maid of honor, best man, personal attendants, and your parents.

Phillip Bag

This gift bag is a gift in itself, but when you fill it up, it's a personalized gem.

Materials

Organza bag with ribbon drawstring
2 or more beads

Step 1: Untie the knots at the end of the drawstring ribbons.

Step 2: Thread beads onto the ribbon.

Step 3: Retie the knots.

Step 4: Fill the bag with the receiver's favorite wine, candy, coffee . . .

Quick & Easy Ideas

❧ Tie a commercially made beaded ribbon around a bottle of wine.

❧ If you're already making bouquet additions (page 50), make a few extra, give them to your florist, and ask her to use them in a bouquet you'll use as a gift.

❧ Make a one-stop bead shop visit and buy a special bead for each person on your special thank-you list. Think beautiful lampworked, carved tagua nut, handmade silver, or antique Bakelite beads. Buy beads that remind you of each intended receiver or just buy the same type of bead for everyone on the list. String each bead on a ribbon that has a brief thank-you note attached.

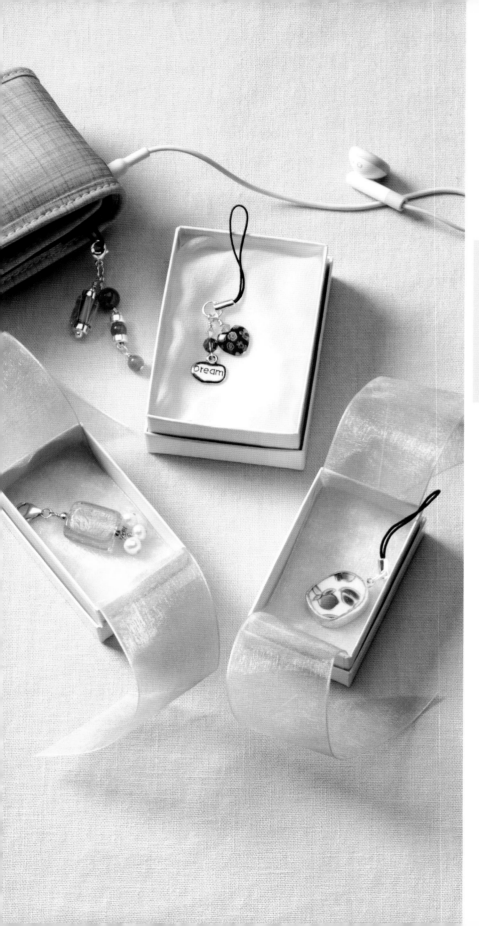

Lucky Charms

This multipurpose charm is a snap to make and a great gift for either women or men. They can be used as a zipper pull or a cell phone decoration (if the phone has the proper attachment ring). They can also be clipped onto a purse, backpack, key ring, or pair of scissors.

Materials and Tools

Beads and charms of your choice

22-gauge or larger head pin(s)

Cell phone finding or large lobster claw clasp with jump ring

Chain-nose pliers

Round-nose pliers

Wire cutters

Step 1: String beads on a head pin in a pleasing design.

Step 2: Make a wrapped loop (see page 12) to secure the beads. Set aside.

Step 3: Open the cell phone charm or lobster claw's ring.

Step 4: Add the dangles to the ring and close it.

Quick & Easy Ideas

✿ String your initial set of beads on an eye pin instead of a head pin and then add other dangles to the eye pin's loop. Or simply add a pendant to the findings.

We're Pinned! Frame

This frame is a special memento of your wedding day and a great gift for parents. When you shop for the frame, consider the interior style and colors of the receiver's home so they actually set it out for all to see!

Materials and Tools
Stuffed fabric frame
Straight sewing pins
Sequins in various sizes
Seed beads
Wedding photo
Measuring tape
Pencil

Step 1: Determine the beaded design you want for the frame. You can carefully measure and mark the places you want the beads to go, or simply work free-form. In any case, if you make a mistake, you can usually repin the beads as necessary without making a mark in the fabric.

Step 2: String beads and sequins onto a pin. It doesn't matter in what order the beads and sequins are strung, but it helps to put on a seed bead first to secure the other beads. It also helps visually if the largest sequins are placed last.

Step 3: Stick the pin into the frame at an angle at the first point in your design. It's important to put the pin in at an angle; this way the pin has a less likely chance of falling out.

Step 4: Continue adding beaded pins to the frame to finish your design.

Step 5: Add the photo.

Bead-Encrusted Photo Album

Jodi Reeb-Myers

This project helps you add a bit of panache to an otherwise run-of-the-mill wedding album. Fill the album with photos from your wedding, and it's a great gift for anyone who attended.

Materials and Tools

Photo album
⅜" Terrifically Tacky Tape
Seed beads; pearl and clear white
Scissors

Step 1: Attach Terrifically Tacky Tape around the opening in the album cover to create a frame.
Step 2: Sprinkle the tape with various clear and pearl seed beads.

Stylin' Girl Thank-You Necklace

Jodi Reeb-Myers

Give this thank-you card to your flower girl, and she'll get a sweet thank-you gift at the same time!

Materials and Tools

Decorative paper
1/8" hole punch
Jeweled flower brad
Flower charms
18" ball chain with clasp
"Thank You" and flower inking stamps
Rose and eggplant inks
5/8" Velcro circle
Scissors

Step 1: Cut decorative paper into a tri-fold purse shape.

Step 2: Punch holes into the paper where the purse strap will go.

Step 3: String flower charms on the beaded chain and thread the chain through the holes.

Step 4: Stamp flowers and "Thank You" on the inside of the purse.

Step 5: Push the brad into the purse flap.

Step 6: Attach the Velcro circle to the inside of the purse flap so you cover the brad.

Bloomin' Bookmark and Thank-You Note

Jodi Reeb-Myers

Anyone in your bridal party would love to receive this special card that not only says, "Thank you," but reminds them of your special day every time they use it as a bookmark.

Materials and Tools

Lavender, cream, and burgundy cardstocks
Lavender ink
Flowerpot inking stamp
Bugle and seed beads
Vellum
Thread
Sheer ribbon
Double-sided tape
1/4" hole punch
Scissors

Step 1: Make a card using the lavender cardstock. Set aside.

Step 2: Stamp the images onto the cream cardstock.

Step 3: String seed and bugle beads on thread and wind the strand around the stamped image.

Step 4: Layer the image on the lavender, then burgundy cardstock to create bookmark. Adhere them all together with tape.

Step 5: Punch a hole at the top of the bookmark and tie the ribbon through the hole.

Step 6: Sew a vellum pocket on the card for the bookmark to fit into.

Bloomin' Bookmark and Thank-You Note

Stylin' Girl Thank-You Necklace

Friendship Gift Tin and Book

Jodi Reeb-Myers

This little piece serves as both a thank-you and a gift for a special person involved in your wedding.

Materials and Tools

Recycled metal tin
Decorative papers
Yarn
Seed beads
Small glass pearl
26-gauge silver wire
Acrylic paint
Flower punch
¼" hole punch
1¼" circle punch
Scissors

Step 1: Decorate the tin by painting it in complementary colors and attaching stamped decorative papers and flowers to the cover with glue. String wire with seed beads and pearls and bend it to create a flower shape. Glue the flower to the cover of the tin as well.

Step 2: Create a small book to fit into the tin by binding a series of stamped decorative papers with holes punched near the edges with yarn. For the cover, punch a circle through the cover and fill with another circle tied with yarn. Embellish the cover with stamps and fill the book with photos or quotes.

The Perfect Dress Memory Book

Jodi Reeb-Myers

The idea of making a memory book for your mom or maid-of-honor is a good one, but an even better idea is to drop the hint for them to make one for you! The basic idea is to share one memory you had with the other person surrounding your wedding.

First, cut an 8" × 8" piece of cardstock to act as the backing for the back of the book. Glue and/or sew various decorative papers, fabrics, photos, scraps (and of course, beads!) to the cardstock. Make pages with more cardstock and decorate those as well. Bind the pages to the back of the book by using small hinges and eyelets.

Materials and Tools
for the Memory Book shown

Tan cardstock

Decorative papers

Beaded hearts and wedding dress

Vintage buttons

Thread

Vellum

Magic Mesh

Barbie doll dress pattern

Vintage brads

Antique copper hinges and eyelets

Ribbon

Sheer fabric

Beaded ribbon

Kraft cardstock

Vintage leaf and flower stamps

Creamy Carmel ink

Pewter wedding plaques

Tin spiral bank

Olive ink

To Someone Special

suppliers

Anna Griffin Inc.
www.annagriffin.com
(888) 817-8170
  Luscious vintage-inspired decorative papers to use for beautifying invitations and thank-you notes.

Art Beads
www.artbeads.com
(866) 715-2323
  A great one-stop online shop for crystals, findings, and all kinds of other beady must-haves.

Bazzill Papers Inc.
www.bazillbasics.com
(480) 558-8557
  Manufacturer of wonderful cardstock—a great base for your paper goods.

The Bead Goes On
www.beadgoeson.com
(866) 861-2323
  Really fantastic Thai silver. The owner is very hands-on, so there's a whole lotta love there.

Beadalon
www.beadalon.com
(866) 423-2325
  They are big and bold and have a successful brand of beading wire named just after them—go figure! (Use the website to find a dealer near you.)

Beads of La Jolla
5645 La Jolla Blvd.
La Jolla, CA 92037
(858) 459-6134
  Arlene shops and teaches here—I guess it's the cat's pajamas!

Fire Mountain Gems
www.firemountaingems.com
(800) 355-2137
  An ultimate smorgasbord of anything beaderly. Really.

General Bead
www.genbead.com
(619) 336-0100 (San Diego)
(415) 255-2323 (San Francisco)
  One of the original hip, hippy, happy bead walk-in bead shops in the United States but a nice online catalog, too.

Lacis
www.lacis.com
(510) 843-7178
  These guys sell the purse clasps for Sandi's project, as well as a whole lot of other amazing, hard-to-find needle arts tools and supplies.

Making Memories
www.makingmemories.com
(801) 294-0430
  Fun and funky embellishment papers, tags, brads, and the like to adorn your invitations and thank-you notes.

Soft Flex Company
www.softflexcompany.com
(866) 925-3539
  Supplier of many hard-to-find vintage and vintage-style items, including rhinestones, filigree, and beads.

Stampin' Up
www.stampinup.com
Stamps, stamps, and stamps! Who can get enough?

references

Baker, Arlene. *Beads in Bloom.* Loveland, Colorado: Interweave Press, 2000.

Campbell, Jean. *Getting Started Stringing Beads.* Loveland, Colorado: Interweave Press, 2005.

De Jong-Kramer, E. *Classic Beaded Purse Patterns.* Kenthurst, N.S.W.: Kangaroo Press, 1996.

Durant, Judith, and Jean Campbell. *The New Beader's Companion.* Loveland, Colorado: Interweave Press, 2005.

Pierce, Don. *Beading on a Loom.* Loveland, Colorado: Interweave Press, 1999.

Sako, Takako. *Bead Weaving Accessories.* Berkeley, California: Lacis, 1998.

Index